G000160677

Yes

in the 1980s

Stephen Lambe
with
David Watkinson

sonicbondpublishing.com

Sonicbond Publishing Limited
www.sonicbondpublishing.co.uk
Email: info@sonicbondpublishing.co.uk

First Published in the United Kingdom 2021
First Published in the United States 2021

British Library Cataloguing in Publication Data:
A Catalogue record for this book is available from the British Library

Copyright Stephen Lambe 2021

ISBN 978-1-78952-125-2

Typeset in ITC Garamond & ITC Avant Garde
Printed and bound in England

Graphic design and typesetting: Full Moon Media

DECADES

Yes

in the 1980s

Stephen Lambe
with
David Watkinson

sonicbondpublishing.com

Dedication

Dedicated to the late Chris Squire,
a man born to live in the 1980s

Acknowledgements

Many thanks to David Watkinson for his enthusiasm for
this project and for making his entire 1980s Yes-related
archive available.

Thanks also to my gorgeous wife Gillian Lambe for
allowing me to go AWOL for weekends on end while I
beavered away on this book.

Thanks also to Huw Lloyd-Jones

Special thanks to Kevin Mulryne and Mark Anthony K
of www.yesmusicpodcast.com, plus Jon Dee
and Graeme Stevenson

Cudos and a stiff negroni to Libido Chafe...

DECADES | Yes in the 1980s

Contents

Foreword By David Watkinson

Being a Yes fan in the 1970s was just a joy. But heading into the 1980s, I am not sure I was ready for what that decade gave us all. It certainly provided a surprise or two, and some of those shocks came as a shock to the system for sure.

I followed Yes diligently during the 80s when I was in my 20s. Even though Yes weren't on the front pages of the music papers, the fanzine world was flourishing, and this was the main way to get information in those pre-internet days.

The beginning of the decade saw the *Drama* album arrive from a changed Yes, which was received with a mixture of shock and awe, leaving the classic Yes line-up to the past behind, yet providing a viable future for the band.

Then the evolution of the new Yes music of *90125* sent more shockwaves across the fan world again, creating what has become a silly but engaging and ongoing love-hate relationship for the era amongst Yes fans. The 1970s Yes fans were labelled 'Troopers', after *The Yes Album* track 'Starship Trooper', and the fans of the 80s Yes style and newbies to the band called themselves 'Generators', from the *Big Generator* album. Add Yes West and Yes East to the future fandom chats and you can see why following Yes can be both entertaining and challenging in equal measure.

Gradually I learned to embrace *Drama*, yet straight away, I really loved the new Yes of *90125*. I was disappointed with Yes for not touring the UK with the *Big Generator* and yet I was delighted with ABWH for their uplifting album and tour in 1989.

The Yes live band in the 80s still gave their fans a wonderful show with spectacular staging. We had Roger Dean stage designs and artwork in 1980 and for the *90125* tour a moving lighting rig, back projections, an elevated stage and Bugs Bunny as an opening act! The shoulder-padded 80s gave us bold hairstyles and costumes that were eye-watering - in particular Chris Squire's. We also had face paint and make up to contend with for the band's videos.

We welcomed Tony Kaye back into the fold, but for the most part, Trevor Rabin was the main creative force during the decade for which I am extremely grateful; Rabin was the catalyst for a change in Yes music and it was an exciting period. The USA saw much more of Yes in that decade than we did in the UK, but the joyful compensation for that was the chance to see Jon Anderson, Rick Wakeman and Asia live shows, and who would have believed the massive success that both Yes and Asia had? It was a delight to see. And from being a fan that enjoyed the elitism of following a prog band in the 1970s, suddenly everyone knew the hit singles: is there anyone who doesn't know 'Owner of a Lonely Heart' or 'Heat of the Moment'?

A downside for the Yes collector through this period was the aesthetics used in the band's cover designs. Without Roger Dean's artwork, the visuals were not as engaging. *Drama* and the *ABWH* albums are strongly integrated with Dean's bold artwork and were joy, whereas, with *90125* and *Big Generator,* there is a lack of connection between the fan, the artwork, and the albums themselves, although an exception to this is the 'Oui' *90125* sweatshirt which I think is still very cool.

1980s Yes - how did it become such a fabulous, frantic decade for them? With more shocking line-up changes, crazy album artwork, huge tours, complex pop songs, a new sense of style and an emphasis on promo videos, Yes managed to storm through the 80s with a fresh spring in their step. They had new members, a clearer vision, played with plenty of energy and joy, and of course, enjoyed massive success. They are Yes, after all, and so we had to expect perpetual change, and looking back, it was all needed to get to the band and fans where we are now.

Welcome to the fabulous 1980s incarnation of Yes, then. A theme that continued on from the decade before is that it's always really been about great music such as 'Into the Lens', 'Hearts', 'Changes', 'Shoot High, Aim Low', 'Rhythm of Love', and 'Brother of Mine'. Maybe after reading this book, it will encourage you to take another look at and listen to the 80s Yes, and perhaps, if you don't already, you will learn to appreciate this colourful, complex, and varied decade of Yes music.

Oh, you don't have an 80s haircut to do it!

David Watkinson, September 2021

Introduction

A vast amount has been written about the Yes of the 1970s, particularly the period 1971 to 1978 when what many people,including your author, believe the band were at their adventurous peak. But what happened next, and for the next ten years, is the subject of this book. It's a fascinating period, both musically but also politically. A band that – despite a few lineup changes along the way – remained relatively stable in the 1970s suffered several severe shocks in the challenging decade that followed.

While Yes – the band - released just three albums during those years, there was some astonishing music from its members as part of other projects, not to mention a fair few that fall into the 'it seemed like a good idea at the time' category, as they attempted to find paths for themselves in a decade in which they often felt forgotten.

With the band on the rocks at the start of 1980, nobody could have predicted what would take place over the next decade. Taking as its basis the fortunes of the five members of the band as it was – officially at least – on January 1 1980, we'll track the albums that Yes made during the decade, as well as the genesis of a fourth full band 'almost-Yes' album at the end of those years. We'll also follow the other fortunes of those five musicians across the ten years, particularly as they were all to reconvene in 1990 as an eight-piece supergroup, and we will welcome four other musicians in and out of the fold during that time: Trevor Horn, Geoff Downes, Trevor Rabin and a returning Tony Kaye. Other musicians that played a part in that era – like Eddie Jobson, Billy Sherwood, Tony Levin, Casey Young and another returning bandmate in Bill Bruford – will also get a well-deserved look in.

For some of these nine musicians – particularly Jon Anderson and Steve Howe – the decade was as busy outside Yes as it was for them within the band. Anderson enjoyed a stop-start solo career and a couple of big chart hits with Greek keyboard player Vangelis, while Steve Howe had success with both Asia and GTR. For Rick Wakeman, the 1980s were more difficult, but he emerged from it a stronger man and a more successful musician. Horn and Downes – although fleeting members of the band itself – remained associated with it one way or another for the better part of the decade. However, other members – particularly Chris Squire, Alan White, Trevor Rabin and Tony Kaye – have careers within this ten-year period built rather more specifically around the fortunes of the band itself.

Most significantly, of the five musicians that began 1980 as members of the band, four were able to repurpose their playing for a more straightforward, but massively more lucrative age. Only Wakeman really struggled. After all, he was a virtuoso musician in an era that fundamentally distrusted such virtuosity. Where was he without that Wakeman 'style'? Howe and Squire were able to play in a more simple fashion and still make it work, but simplicity just didn't suit the beleaguered ivory tinkler.

A fair amount has been written about the decade by the members themselves. Rick Wakeman and Steve Howe have covered the period in their autobiographies, as has Bill Bruford, while Yes chroniclers Chris Welch, David Watkinson and Alan Farley have also discussed the decade in a bit of detail. The two Trevors – Rabin and Horn – have also spoken extensively about their involvement in the band during this time. Alan White discusses the period from time to time, although his testimony is variable and usually highly diplomatic. Jon Anderson has an autobiography in the works, although if the first chapter that appeared in 2019 is anything to go by, it may gloss over gory detail. Sadly, the death of Chris Squire in 2015 means that we only have his public utterances, which were usually couched in a certain amount of diplomacy, to go on.

Piecing together the 'facts' of this period is not as easy as it might seem. While I have no doubt that there's any intention to stretch the truth from any particular protagonist, viewpoints do differ, even on some points of fact. As can occur in life generally, we tend to see situations from our own perspectives, filtered through our own biases, which can lead to slight exaggerations or an emphasis on viewpoints that favour our own agendas. This is as true of members of the band as it is with the testimony of some of the key support players during the decade, like Atlantic executive Phil Carson and the band's manager Brian Lane. Differing perspectives are rife throughout the Yes story, particularly in the complex and political 1980s. However, with some creative reading between the lines, some sort of approximation is possible.

The purpose of this book, therefore, is to tie all the various threads together to provide a musical biography of the band and its members across the decade. It is quite a complex tale with many solo releases to mention (and a fair few to pass over fleetingly), but we will take as the core of the book the twists and the turns, the triumphs and the tragedies, that befell the band itself during this turbulent decade. In parallel, we'll track the musical journeys of all those individual musicians that played a part in this often almost unbelievable story.

Although the five musicians that comprised the band at the start of 1980 will provide the backbone of the book, three other figures, in particular, influenced the fortunes of the band throughout the decade. We must not forget the influence of the two Trevors, of course – Messrs. Horn and Rabin. Horn features prominently in the stories of all three 'official' Yes albums during the 1980s, firstly as vocalist (and de facto producer) of *Drama*, then as the producer of *90125* and finally the first producer of *Big Generator*. Rabin – that great, benign control freak – is, without doubt, the most important figure in the creation of those latter two albums.

However, another name crops up from time to time during the course of this story. This figure is a shadowy one, but his influence cannot be underestimated. Brian Lane was Yes' Manager during the *Drama* era and remained involved in the fortunes of Squire, White and Howe as they tried to find their ways in new bands after the 1981 split. He was intimately involved (you might even say 'to blame') in the formations of Asia, GTR and ABWH. It's also notable that he was NOT involved in Cinema and the construction of the 1983 version of Yes. Lane's role in this (for want of a better word) 'drama' is somewhat veiled but cannot be underestimated. A former record plugger before moving into band management, he did the deals and exercised his powers of persuasion on the creatives, for better or for worse. Lane does not appear as a talking head in either of the Yes video documentaries, but he has been interviewed about this period, so we'll tap into his voice from time to time.

Finally, while Lane plays an important part in our story, another – somewhat less shadowy – 'suit' also has a major part to play. Phil Carson at Atlantic records had been involved in the fortunes of the band throughout the 1970s, and, as we shall see, it was he that introduced Chris Squire to Trevor Rabin; it was he that suggested Tony Kaye join the new band, and it was he that manoeuvred Jon Anderson back into the band in 1983. It's clear that from a very early stage – probably as soon as Cinema formed – Carson envisaged a new version of Yes. Whatever his motives – commercial and sentimental, one suspects – he's an important figure/

The Lead Singer Problem

If this book has a theme, it is the importance to any ambitious and successful band to have the best lead singer possible – both in the eyes of the group itself and the 'suits' that might be putting up the money that allows the band to exist. Throughout the 1970s, Yes did not have a problem in this regard. Whether you love or hate his voice (and if you're reading this book, there's a strong chance that you love it), there is no doubt that Jon Anderson is a great lead vocalist. When he left the band at the start of 1980, the band were – in a sense at least – lucky, in that a decent – if inexperienced - singer fell into their laps, in Trevor Horn. The problem arose when he was required to demonstrate his talents in front of thousands of people.

When the band splintered further at the start of 1981, this problem remained. Steve Howe's new project Asia chose John Wetton – a fine but unconventional lead singer – against the initial wishes of the band's label Geffen and their management team, headed by Brian Lane. The band stood fast, and made the arrangement work. For a while, at least.

Meanwhile, Chris Squire and Alan White had formed Cinema with whizz kid Trevor Rabin. Slightly uncomfortably, this new band had two potential lead vocalists in Squire and Rabin. Although Squire has taken the odd short lead vocal throughout his career – he was the original vocalist when the band played the 'Dissolution' section of 'Starship Trooper' as part of another song 'For Everyone' as early as 1969 – he had usually done so reluctantly, with good reason. He's an excellent harmony vocalist, but there's a timbre to his voice that doesn't please everyone. So too Rabin, whose voice is pleasing but boyish, with a tendency to strain on higher notes. Record companies, understandably, felt uneasy about either musician fronting a band with this level of commercial ambition. The management/record company pressure to bring back Jon Anderson – even if both Squire and Rabin (arguably) felt uneasy about this – was understandable.

When Howe moved on from Asia and formed GTR with Steve Hackett, there was no question of either guitarist singing, so former Nightwish vocalist Max Bacon was brought in. Bacon is very much a *lead* vocalist with a record company-pleasing, clean, high register voice that could handle AOR-style material but (if we're brutally honest) he lacks a huge amount of the character needed to make him a great, as opposed to a good, singer.

As our story ends, with Anderson once again out of the band, the remaining members (or Yes West as they have often been called) had the same old problem. They were a band looking to find a vocalist 'like' Anderson, without having Anderson himself.

Indeed, there are many 'what ifs' as Yes wound their unsteady way through the 1980s, and most of these revolve around the presence – or lack thereof – of Anderson in the band. What is certain is that even when he was absent, the band never quite shook off his influence. In 1982 and 1983, Squire and Rabin could have bitten the bullet and brought in another singer at any time. But they didn't – they returned to their mercurial vocalist.

1979 and all that...

It had all started so well.

When Rick Wakeman officially rejoined Yes at the end of 1976, it had felt like a new beginning. The band – using Wakeman as a session player – had recorded *Going For The One* at Mountain Studios in Montreux, Switzerland. To all of the musicians involved, the band seemed rejuvenated and happy to be recording together again after a break of two years. The album was a big success, as was the four-month world tour to promote it. Yet cracks began to show when the band reconvened to record *Tormato* at the rather more familiar Advison Studios in London. This was, for many fans, a patchy and confused affair. With Wakeman now recording as a full-time member and requiring an equal place in the mix to Steve Howe – and no producer to mediate between everyone – the end result was somewhat mixed, although much beloved of a significant subgroup of Yes supporters to this day. Ironically, it could be argued that what the band probably needed at that point was an 'ideas' producer – one who could lend a hand with arrangements, such as Bob Ezrin or – as he was yet to become – Trevor Horn.

Nonetheless, the resulting tour, which took the band well into 1979 over two legs, was another huge success. However, auspices were not good when the band finally convened to record the next album in Paris in 1979. There were several problems.

Firstly, the band seemed to be splitting into two camps that were pulling in different directions. Steve Howe, Chris Squire and Alan White were in one camp while Jon Anderson and Rick Wakeman comprised the other. Attempts to record each other's material produced little enthusiasm, as is shown by the pieces that have appeared from those sessions both through official and unofficial channels. It seems that neither the hotels the band were staying in near the studios nor the producer somewhat imposed on the band – the prestigious but eccentric Roy Thomas Baker – passed much muster. Furthermore, years of inter-band financial issues were coming home to roost, with sales of *Tormato,* in particular, showing a distinct slump. An agreement was reached within the band regarding a 'levelling up' of the group's finances. But it was an uneasy truce, hardly conducive to the recording of top-quality music.

Rick Wakeman, in his 1995 autobiography *Say Yes,* suggests that the split that occurred that Winter was pretty cut and dried. He reports that he and Jon Anderson made the decision to quit while drinking Calvados in a café opposite the studio in Paris. However, it seems that the decision to leave was not quite so final, and in reality, another truce was agreed. However, when Alan White broke his ankle roller skating with Richard Branson (if White ever writes an autobiography, there's the title, right there) and was unable to play his drums as a result, this may well have been a blessing in disguise, and recording halted. The band agreed to reconvene in the new year in London.

1980 – A Year of Drama

On January 1 1980, the official lineup of Yes was Jon Anderson, Chris Squire, Steve Howe, Alan White and Rick Wakeman, as it had been since the end of 1976. This wasn't just a band in name only. After the lack of respect and creativity that had blighted the Paris sessions had been tempered by White's broken ankle, the whole band – at the behest of worried manager Brian Lane – had returned to their respective homes to cool off over Christmas and reconvene in London. A small rehearsal space had been hired at Redan Recorders in Queensway, London (which closed in 1991 and is now offices). While the rift between the two factions of the band – Anderson and Wakeman on one side, Squire, Howe and White on the other – had not been healed, there was hope that a solution might be reached, and an album salvaged.

In his autobiography *All My Yesterdays,* Steve Howe reports that Jon did finally make an appearance at the rehearsal studio to play the three musicians that were there (Wakeman never showed at all) some of the songs that he had been working on while he had been away in Paris. Howe doesn't report any animosity between them but does suggest that the musical divisions that had been apparent in Paris the previous autumn had not been rectified. Jon's songs were sweet, simple and folky, with sing-along choruses and major key progressions. Meanwhile, the three musicians who had turned up to rehearse were working as a guitar-based power trio, playing with fire and complexity. Anderson, says Howe, left that day and they didn't see him again. The three-piece played on...

Out with the old, in with the new

It's not quite clear *precisely* how and why Jon and Rick finally came to leave the band, despite a fair amount of column inches devoted to it in books about Yes, and the various comments and reports detailed above. We know that the two camps were unhappy with each other in Paris, and that there were also ongoing arguments about the way that money that the band had earned had been divided up. Chris Welch suggests that the fundamental schism over finances was probably between Jon Anderson and Steve Howe, though it's probable that Chris Squire, whose lifestyle was never less than hedonistic and possibly even Alan White, had some part to play, one way or the other. Indeed, the rot had been setting in for some years, with no album since *Close To The Edge* had been designated platinum in the key markets of Britain and the USA, although *Tormato,* of all albums, finally achieved that status in the USA – possibly due to the mammoth tour which promoted it.

In the *Yes Classic Artists* DVD, Jon gives a couple of reasons, one of which has an air of inevitability about it:

> I think everyone fell out with each other. I think everyone was tired of each other. It happens every ten years. It's only natural. You spend so much time with each other. I knew the band better than I knew my children. That's tough. After a while, you realise you're not balancing things very well.

Yet at the same time, he also suggests that there were musical issues that may have come from within the band but also from Atlantic, saying: 'I'd just had enough of being told we weren't selling enough records, [that] we weren't doing the right music.'

There's no doubt that the financial aspects of the band were a major point for Steve, although he's understandably a bit vague about who was to blame and precisely how they were resolved. He dissects the psychology behind this in his autobiography, in a series of paragraphs that, while vague, sum up some of the politics that exist in any band, and the crutch that 'management' can often provide on a band where internal communication is breaking down:

> About half the breakups were musical. But others had much more complex causes – a mixture of personality clashes, financial disagreements and leadership challenges. There were those who may have believed they ran, controlled or directed Yes. But if they did, they were only fooling themselves. There have always been loud voices and quieter voices in Yes, confrontational or non-confrontational members. Officially the band was/is a democracy where each vote counts and the majority wins.
>
> The politics of rock bands are loathed by all, yet they determined many an outcome. Someone might so vehemently disagree with the planned idea that we had to respect their individual feelings and hold back. We could each then refuse to accept a particular plan, assuming it wasn't just one person disagreeing with what was being offered. Management would have to vote, too (how anything was ever agreed is a mystery). There are many individual calls to management discussing the strengths of one argument over another.

This could have been a filter for opinions but became divisive when another member's views were portrayed wrongly. 'He's happy to do that' would be the report, but later from the horse's mouth you would hear, 'I don't want to do that'. Inconsistencies would repeatedly upset us, causing certain people's reputations to become tarnished. Who could we trust? We were learning different things from each other but left much to advisers. Our newfound success put us in our own firing line.

The band continued to rehearse as a three-piece at Redan Recorders. It seemed that there was still hope that Jon and Rick would join in, but after Anderson's fleeting appearance these became less and likely, and by the end of March a formal split appears to have taken place. Howe notes, on the *Yes Classic Artists* documentary, that for a while, this was by no means cut and dried, with both musicians giving excuses as to why they didn't appear at the London rehearsals. This also affected the music the threesome were making:

This was when Chris, Alan and I started to write 'Tempus Fugit' and stuff. It was kind of aggressive. And full of angst. We were getting frustrated.

Indeed, the music the three-piece were working on appears to largely comprise fast, aggressive material; 'Tempus Fugit', as Howe has said, was first written at these sessions, as was the untypical, almost punky blues-rock piece 'Go Through This', of which more a little later. As well as a fledgling version of that track, the Rhino remaster of *Drama* also includes 'Track 4 (Satellite)', a rather more waffly affair that might have been distilled into something more interesting had it been given more attention.

But problems were brewing. In anticipation of an album from the Paris sessions, a US tour had been booked for the summer – and it was (supposedly) sold out. Actually, it wasn't, but the key dates, such as Madison Square Gardens, were. These were three musicians in search of a direction and some more material – and time was running out. Meanwhile, in a land far, far away – well, Brick Lane in East London, which is just across London, if we're honest – a keyboard player and a singer were waiting in the wings.

Up until 1979, Trevor Horn and Geoff Downes had both enjoyed the sorts of careers as jobbing musicians that many did during the era. Indeed, neither musician had done much to distinguish themselves from

Above: Jon Anderson was given a *Melody Maker* front page in September 1980. It was the last time he was able to gain such interest from the music press. (*David Watkinson Collection*)

Above: *Drama* was generally well reviewed, as it is here by Brian Harrigan of *Melody Maker*. (*David Watkinson Collection*)

hundreds of others finding their feet in the music industry of the 1970s. Horn had played sessions as a bassist, including on the sort of cheaply produced compilation albums (often part of the *Top Of The Pops* series) that had also given musicians like Elton John experience in a recording studio. He also did some production work and recorded radio and TV jingles. Later in the decade, he acted as a musical director and as a songwriter for hire without ever becoming really successful. Downes, on the other hand, had played in a variety of bands, including one called She's French and he was also in fusion guitarist Gary Boyles' band. He and Horn met when they both auditioned to be in British singer Tina Charles' touring group. They also went on to form a short-lived British disco outfit called Chromium (or Chrome in the USA) which also featured composer Anne Dudley, with Horn as producer.

In 1977 the duo began writing songs alongside guitarist Bruce Woolley. The music that the as-yet-unnamed band were playing was sparkier, more in keeping with the late 1970s new wave-influenced zeitgeist. In 1979 the band signed to Island Records and at this point Woolley departed, to form his own band, The Camera Club, although he co-wrote 'Video Killed The Radio Star'. The name 'The Buggles' was a parody of 'The Beatles', and was intended to be absurd, as the band was never intended to be more than a studio project. The Buggles were always intended to be partially satirical – their music a concept album based around the effects of technology on society, but unashamedly 'pop' in character, and with a strong nostalgic aspect. Was it really 'new wave'? Not really, but it's understandable why that label was felt appropriate at the time, in an era when 'labels' were all-important.

The Buggles: The Age Of Plastic

Personnel:
Geoff Downes: production, keyboards, synthesizers, drums and percussion programming, vocoder
Trevor Horn: production, vocals, bass guitar, guitar, synthesizers, programming
Dave Birch: guitars
Richard James Burgess: drums
Tina Charles: background vocals
Debi Doss and Linda Jardim: background vocals on 'Video Killed the Radio Star'
Paul Robinson: drums
Bruce Woolley: guitar
Gary Langan: mixer, vocal recording

Bob Ludwig: Mastering
Hugh Padgham: engineer, instrumental recording
Recorded at Virgin's Town House, West London, Sarm East Studios, Brick Lane, London
Highest chart places: UK: 27, USA: Did not chart
All tracks are written by The Buggles, except 'Video Killed the Radio Star' and 'Clean, Clean', which are by Horn/Downes/Woolley
Track list: 1. Living in the Plastic Age 2. Video Killed the Radio Star 3. Kid Dynamo 4. I Love You (Miss Robot) 5. Clean, Clean 6. Elstree 7. Astroboy (And the Proles on Parade) 8. Johnny on the Monorail

Although it was released three months before the duo joined Yes, it's worth an in-depth look at *The Age Of Plastic*, since, although very much following the stylistic ethic of the new wave as we've discussed, it does give some clues as to what they brought to this brief incarnation of Yes. Indeed, the four videos that Horn and Downes recorded for the album – especially the two biggest-selling singles 'Video Killed The Radio Star' and 'Living In The Plastic Age' – also give plenty of clues as to the 'leanings' of the duo.

Although it doesn't appear first on the album – it's sequenced second – 'Video' is the only track from the record to have seeped into the public consciousness worldwide. It was a number one hit in the UK (for just one week in late October 1979) and in various other territories across Europe. Its ubiquity in the USA was to come, as it was used as the opening track on the launch of MTV on 1 August 1981. There's no doubt that despite the ironic nature of the lyrics, it was the subject of the song – the triumph of video over sound as a way of digesting music – rather than its quality in itself, that gave it that unexpected boost on MTV.

It does have 'hit' written all over it, full as it is with sonic tricks, from Horn's treated vocals (used throughout the song, rather than for part of it) and its sing-song, nursery rhyme-style refrain. The song – and the video that accompanied it – is a piece of stylized kitsch, very much 'of its time'. If you heard this song in isolation – and millions did – you might consider the band to be a bubblegum pop outfit. The track is so extreme, in a sense, that it almost tips into 'novelty song' territory, a genre particularly well-loved in the UK. This was the truth behind the horrified reaction of many fans when the duo joined Yes. It wasn't just that these were purveyors of vacuous pop; worse, this was a *novelty* band. Sacrilege.

We were wrong, of course. Even in those first view videos, there was something about that keyboard player (particularly) that promised something different. Downes' rig appeared to be very 'prog'. This was not one guy playing a Prophet 5 in the back of the shot – this guy had a whole rig and he was actually playing them, sometimes two different instruments on either sides of him. 'He looks a bit like Rick Wakeman', we thought, 'and he plays a bit like him too!' This was promising, surely? At the end of the video was a short instrumental break, and – look, the singer has strapped on a bass and it looks like he can actually play it!

The opening track and second single, 'Living In The Plastic Age' starts unpromisingly – its verse has Horn singing in a mockney accent, while bass and keyboards ape the disco style so popular at the time. Indeed, if this is reminiscent of anyone with its synth trills, it's later-period Abba. However, the operatic vocals provide interest and when the song moves to its chorus, it comes to life, with Horn singing in a more 'natural' voice and his songwriting moving beyond the new wave influence towards something a little more timeless. There's a proggy lead synth and an atmospheric twelve-string guitar that could come straight out of 'Machine Messiah'.

Opening with bubbly bass and Fender Rhodes as if it were the intro to a Level 42 song, 'Kid Dynamo' morphs into something of a rocker, albeit not quite so successfully. The 'Kid Dynamo' refrain soon becomes a bit tedious, as do Horn's heavily treated vocals. However, the closer to side one, 'I Love You (Miss Robot)', works rather better, driven by Horn's expertly played slap bass and Downes' Vocoder refrain. Despite the effects, the quality of the song shines through, and underneath, it's an excellent slice of soul pop.

Side two opens with the other two – less successful – singles from the album. Again, 'Clean Clean' is a decent song rather buried in novelty, particularly Horn's cod-American accent. Aside from another somewhat insistent chorus, it has some nods towards art pop, and an arrangement strongly influenced by 10CC. 'Elstree', however, is one of the best songs on the album. Had it not been the fourth single, with the law of diminishing returns kicking in, one suspects that it might have performed rather better. It's splendidly catchy, but in a good way, and while Horn's treated vocals remain, he sings 'naturally' on the chorus and the arrangement is shorn of too many contemporary ticks, giving the song a timeless quality missing from much of the album. Downes' contributions here are largely his staccato piano – a feature of the whole album – plus strings and some neo-classical synth. It's both a good, catchy song and something that that has many hints of the band's prog leanings.

Such leanings also come across on the next track, 'Astroboy', another song that is allowed to breathe despite some kitsch touches. Horn's vocals sound most like they do on *Drama*, here and his bass playing is the closest to Chris Squire on the album. There are genuine melodic suggestions of 'Machine Messiah' at times, and while the smooth refrain, with its finely integrated female vocals, is very 'pop', elsewhere there are hints of what was to come. 'Johnny On the Monorail' – which closes the album – acts as a sort of a summary of what has gone before it, throwing female voices, some proggy keys and an up-tempo arrangement into an impressive final track. There's even a somewhat progressive mid-section, featuring acoustic guitar and piano, before the song itself chugs back in for an expended coda, featuring some lead synth and almost heavy metal guitar.

What does this album tell us? Firstly, it demonstrates that Horn and Downes were no novelty artists. There's a great deal of contemporary (and somewhat dated) stylisation on the album, but strip that away and there are some great songs, very much in an art pop vein. Downes is very much the 'featured' instrumentalist throughout and while he doesn't play anything requiring a huge amount of dexterity, his keyboard palette is impressive. While it is largely based largely around piano and synths, his wide usage of various styles of synthetic instrumentation is deeply impressive. When Yes hired Wakeman in 1971, it was partially because of his willingness to embrace new technology, and while he had attempted to continue this process into the late 70s, he had largely backed the wrong horses – the Polymoog (an early analogue polysynth) and Birotron (an advance on the Mellotron) being cases in point. Downes had a foot in each era – a trained musician with a deep interest in progressive rock, he was also up to date with the new range of polysynths and with the Fairlight and Synclavier both entering production around this time – albeit at extortionate prices – his willingness to absorb this sort of technology was definitely in his favour.

The Yuggles Are Born

The exact circumstances around the recruitment of Horn and Downes into Yes seem fairly clear, although perspectives do very a bit. While these viewpoints are not exactly contradictory, they do muddy the waters. However, it seems that Horn and Downes – having sold a lot of copies of 'Video' across Europe – decided that they needed some sort of representation. Horn takes up the story on the *Yes Classic Artists* DVD:

> We needed a manager. My wife had been working with someone who was being managed by a guy called Brian Lane. I was aware that Brian Lane was the manager of Yes, because I'd seen his name on the album sleeves. At first, he had seemed like an amusing, interesting person, and my wife said, 'you should meet this guy. He could be the right manager for you'. So, we met Brian and there's no doubt that when you first meet him at lunch, he's a real character. So, for our sins, Geoffrey and I decided to have Brian manage us for The Buggles. Anyway, it turned out to not be a very clever move for us. But it brought us into contact with the guys from Yes.

Meanwhile, the remaining three-piece were still rehearsing and looking for a direction. With that US tour booked for August, something needed to happen – and it needed to happen fast. Lane – now the manager of The Buggles – suggested that the duo write a song for Yes, who were lacking material. 'Fly From Here' was deemed appropriate, and Horn visited Squire at his home, New Piper's in Virginia Water in Surrey, and played it for him. Initially, Squire was somewhat coy about the whereabouts of Anderson and Wakeman. But it was also at this point that Squire noticed that Horn's voice was not a million miles away from Anderson's. Spotting a golden opportunity, he started working on Horn to get him to become the band's new singer. Horn was horrified to begin with. There he was – a massive Yes fan, and now he was about to become their vocalist. 'It was such a wild idea', he said in a contemporary interview with *Circus* magazine. He wasn't wrong. The five musicians met up at Redan Recorders and started playing together, initially for a two-week trial period. Thus, by stealth, they were they brought into the band. Chris Squire – who by this point was running the band if anyone was – needed to do some persuasion, particularly with Steve Howe, who was wary of the two musicians pop leanings as he felt they might not fit into the Yes aesthetic. But Howe also saw the benefits:

> In 1980, the new lineup presented us with a golden opportunity to reset our business structure and make a break with the past. Good teamwork and shared writing meant we were beginning to chart the groups direction and reinstating its standards.

Squire also had a new vision for the band, which was to take the group back to 'the old days' – a point in time, perhaps in 1971 – when the original vision that he had with Jon Anderson was still being followed. This informed many of the decisions taken in the creation of *Drama* – good and bad. The band's manager Brian Lane had a different perspective, however, telling Daryl Easlea of *Prog* magazine in 2016:

> In 1979, I took on the management of The Buggles, again a one-off – the first video on MTV – but there was unrest in the Yes camp. I was in hospital having surgery and the following happened: Chris Squire, Steve Howe and Alan White took it upon themselves to fire Jon. Rick then left the band in sympathy. I got out of hospital and discovered they had appointed Trevor Horn as the new lead singer and Geoff Downes as the new keyboard player. Overnight, 'Yes' had become 'Maybe'.

Another tidbit from the era provided by Chris Welch in his autobiography of the band is that 'Fly From Here' was demoed with the assistance of Bill Bruford on drums, as Squire wanted to work with him again. Whether this is the version of the song that appears on the expanded edition of the second Buggles album *Adventures In Modern Recording* is not clear, although no credits are given for this track. It doesn't sound like Squire or Bruford and may be a well-programmed drum machine, but given the 'at best tarted up demo' quality of the recording, it's difficult to be certain.

One decision that didn't work was to bring back Eddie Offord to produce the album. The now-five piece fledgling band had moved from Redan to The Townhouse Studio is Shepherds Bush, then owned by Richard Branson. Offord had effectively been the sixth member of the band until *Relayer* in 1974, but he had struggled with addiction on the road, and the spring of 1980 found him in something of a 'different place' as a person, personified by a certain level of eccentricity and unreliability. In his autobiography, Howe reports Offord's hilarious attempts to cook a London pigeon in the studio kitchen. After three weeks of little more than partial attendance at the sessions, Offord was fired. This was a setback to Squire's attempt to relive the band's 1970s glories, but the band were not unduly inconvenienced since his replacement was Hugh Padgham. While the engineer's glory days – with Kate Bush and Phil Collins particularly – were still ahead of him, there's no doubting his professionalism and skill. With Horn largely producing on behalf of the band, the real work began.

Drama

Personnel:

Trevor Horn: vocals, bass

Chris Squire: bass, piano, vocals

Steve Howe: guitar, vocals

Alan White: drums, percussion, vocals

Geoff Downes: keyboards and vocoder

Written, arranged and produced by Yes.

Backing tracks produced by Eddie Offord.

Recorded at the Town House, London, April to June 1980.

Engineer Hugh Padgham. Mixed at Sarm Studios.

Highest chart places: UK: 2, USA: 18.

Tracklisting: 1. Machine Messiah 2. White Car 3. Does It Really Happen 4. Into The Lens 5. Rn Through The Light 6. Tempus Fugit

Once recording began with the two Buggles in May, Squire put his vision for a rebooted Yes into operation. In particular, he encouraged Downes to combine his love of new technology with various references to the early 70s incarnation of the band, thus the proliferation of Hammond organ and, to a lesser extent, Minimoog, on the resulting album. Howe recorded his guitars offsite at RAK studios, partially to save time but partially because – well – we know he prefers that. It was all a big rush, of course, but everyone concerned found the creative process fulfilling. Ideas flowed in from all quarters, and an album quickly took shape.

In May, the bold new lineup was announced in the British music press to the considerable shock of those that still cared. Work continued through May and June, with mixing undertaken at SARM studios by Horn and Howe. Horn got married to his fiancée Jill Sinclair during this time, giving up his planned two-week honeymoon for a weekend in Bournemouth, so he and Howe could complete work. It didn't stop most of the rest of the band from going on holiday, though. This retreat to the tried and trusted also stretched to the cover design, with Roger Dean returning with a striking cover that mixed his famed landscapes with a more stark, moodier edge. The Dean Yes logo stayed, combined with a rather more angular 'Drama'. Yes fans, who do love a conspiracy, have noted that Dean's cover shows three cats chasing away two birds. Hmmm.

As for the recording process, Geoff Downes describes the atmosphere in the studio on the *Yes Classic Artists* DVD:

Once we got into the studio, it was pretty vibrant. We were writing some good music and some pretty complicated music. It was a good time for us. We enjoyed making the album. It was very creative, very productive.

But considering the near panic in which the album was recorded, it's an astonishing piece of work. The material is terrific and considering that Yes had often pieced compositions together over excruciatingly long periods of time, arrangements must have been put together very quickly, and the joins really don't show. Horn should really take a huge amount of credit for his production work, particularly during the mixing stage. We know that he went on to an astonishing career in this area within a few years, but here he showed what a talent he already was.

His vocal performance is good, too, although it's noticeable how prominent Chris Squire's backing vocals are in the mix, with Horn singing completely alone far less often than Anderson might have done. Many have described *Drama* as a 'guitar album', and it's true that with a keyboard player more willing to provide texture rather than leads, there's far more room for Howe to do his 'thing'. In his autobiography, he describes how the parts that he recorded at RAK were treated with displeasure by the rest of the band initially, but later they 'settled in' and only one part – a steel guitar section for 'Into The Lens' nicknamed the 'buzzy bee' – was completely vetoed. Whether the inclusion of all his parts had anything to do with Howe's presence at the mixing stage, of course, has gone unreported. As it is, his playing is superb – aggressive, virtuosic, varied and finely judged. It may just be his best, sustained performance on a Yes album

But for me, this is actually a bass album, if it's anything. Many of the songs – and not only the ones developed when the band were a three piece – are built around quite complex bass parts. Not that Squire had been absent on other albums, of course, but here he dominates as much as Howe. Given that his voice is also all over the album, it's a great, high-energy performance.

Two other influences seem to inform this slight alteration in the band's sonic textures. One was the new wave, of course. We have already discussed that, in a sense, Horn and Downes were slightly 'fraudulent' purveyors of their new wave sound. It wasn't really their natural style, and the sound of The Buggles was more about writing and performing to a concept. However, the energy and styles of that era certainly seeped into the album. Of course, 'Run Through The Light' has more than a little of Sting's vocal style with the Police, but it's there in 'Tempus Fugit' and 'Into The Lens' in more subtle ways.

The other is heavy metal. Again, *Drama* is not a 'heavy' album as such, and if any guitars are distorted, it's only very slightly. That 'Machine Messiah' opens with a big, simple unison passage does not make it feel like a heavy rock track, but it's clear that the burgeoning New Wave Of British Heavy Metal had not gone entirely unnoticed by the band.

There's no doubt that 'Machine Messiah' makes an immediate statement, from Howe's fade-in opening and the simple unison riff, with Downes – in the first minute – giving us the unfamiliar (those orchestral synth groans) and the familiar (the synth that doubles Howe's lead guitar line). The opening vocal section is far more familiar as well, and it's interesting to note that Horn isn't introduced too early – he's one of the ensemble that sings the opening verse. The Church organ also places us on familiar territory, and Horn's lyrics are nicely oblique without being too 'Jon Anderson'. Indeed, the concept of the 'machine messiah' might have come from *The Golden Age Of Plastic*; it feels of a similar sci-fi vintage.

This opening section clips along with high energy and great melodicism. Indeed, the first lead vocal is by Squire, with Horn taking the next line, almost like a formal introduction '...and herrrrre's Trevor!' It's also clear that the arrangement gives space for both Downes and Horn – the Moog lick in the next instrumental section – which is copied, amazingly, by Squire on bass – has Howe accompanying with aggressive, staccato chords, before supplying his own lead line, thick with wah pedal. It's a thrilling section, and descending piano figure returns us to the main riff.

We now get Horn's first proper lead vocal – singing with himself – over stummed twelve string guitar (also his) and Mellotron. A moment of stillness, and the opening vocal section repeats, with added keyboards giving this section even more exuberance; there are shades of 'Seasons Of Man' in the approach, here, with subtle differences in arrangement adding interest to what might otherwise have been a straight repetition. A return to acoustic guitar, the 'Machine Messiah' refrain, and we end on another throb of distorted electric guitar.

The most collaborative piece on the album, and pieced together in a day, it meshes 'old Yes' with some of the textures introduced by the new recruits. Horn was responsible for the verse, whereas the three-piece had the 'heavy' section, with White, in particular, laying claim to the fast Moog and bass passage; how Squire cursed him for its complexity and speed.

It's the clarity of 'Machine Messiah's' arrangement that really impresses – there's real space for everyone – and the subtle key changes are masterful. Overall, it's an astonishing opening and deserves a place alongside 'And You And I' and 'Heart of The Sunrise' as a mid-length Yes classic.

It's no coincidence that *Drama* has structural similarities to *The Yes Album* released in 1971. That album has – in essence – four long pieces with two on each side, divided up by shorter, or if you like, 'bridging' tracks. With 'The Clap' and 'A Venture' doing that job on the 1971 album, 'White Car' does the same thing on side one of *Drama*. This is a short Horn / Downes piece, created mainly on the Fairlight by Downes, but with an added acoustic guitar – which doubles Downes' Asian-inspired melody – and some impressive percussion from White. Horn sings the song solo – although there's a hint that even this short piece may be too high for his natural voice. 'White Car' was to become part of Downes' solo on the tour and took on a life of its own in the December UK shows, when the band sang it as a five-man a cappella piece after the encores as a tribute to John Lennon, who was murdered in New York on 8 December 1980.

Closing side one is the excellent 'Does It Really Happen'. This song had its genesis as a piece from the *Tormato* (or possibly Paris) era, and there's a rudimentary demo of the song with Anderson singing amongst the bonus tracks on the Rhino remaster of that album. While the demo takes a couple of minutes to get going, a fair amount of the song is in place, and enough of the vocal melody for Anderson to be worthy of a songwriting credit that he didn't receive on *Drama* – based on circumstantial evidence, at least. In its finished form, the track is a fine, off-kilter piece. Squire and Horn sing in unison, in the main, another example of Squire sharing the vocal load, while Downes mixes new technology with some terrific Tony Kaye-style Hammond. It's a terrific combination of the new and the old. The 'echo' vocal section and the bold a capella section towards the end of the song are beautifully judged, as is the mallet percussion from White. The synth-led coda, which introduces a bass solo of sorts, is also inspired – there are suggestions of a up-tempo 'Wurm' here.

When we heard 'Into The Lens' for the first time, many of us were a little perturbed. The 'I Am A Camera' refrain – this is the title of the song on the second Buggles album from which this version is derived – was a bit cheesy, surely? Not only does Horn sing this repeatedly, but it's also played on the Vocoder – a voice synthesizer that was already familiar but associated largely with dance music. But we got used to it. Indeed, this is, in a sense, a 'Yesified' cover version in the same way that the band's 1972 version of the Simon and Garfunkel classic 'America' was. Listen to the Buggles version on the expanded version of *Adventures In Modern Recording* and it's the same song – but here given an expansive Yes arrangement. The staccato opening might have come from any Yes album in the 1970s, and Howe delivers his most impressive lead guitar performance of the album. Horn's voice is well suited to this song, and his performance is confident and blends beautifully with Squire's harmony vocal, the latter taking more of a back seat on this track. The arrangement uses an interesting trick of having the same lick played on different instruments – piano (using the bass notes), bass and Howe's Telecaster. The intensity that builds across the track's eight or so minutes is also masterful, driven by White's drumming and the urgency of Howe's lead playing.

'Run Through the Light' is another piece with its roots in another time. The band attempted a version of this song during the Paris sessions in 1979, and it can be heard as 'Dance Through The Light' on the Rhino reissue of *Drama*. It's a full band piece – though very brief – with Anderson singing through some effects, although his vocals are missing from the second half. If this was an attempt by the band to 'go disco' (perish the thought) it sounds uninspiring, with neither White or Squire sounding comfortable in that style, with most of the drive coming from Wakeman's staccato synth chords.

On *Drama*, however, it becomes a different beast entirely. The basic song is retained, but there's less of an attempt to make it 'danceable' and some of the staccato rhythm is provided by Howe's mandolin – not an instrument one associates with disco. Instead, with Horn's vocal melody making him sound like Sting of the Police, his own bass bubbling away (Squire instead plays a barely audible piano) and White's drums recorded using the 'gated' style pioneered by Hugh Padgham, this track becomes the most 'modern' of the six here, and as a result, is the one that had probably dated least well. It's still expertly done, though.

The album goes out with a bang with 'Tempus Fugit'. If any of the pieces on this terrific album have stood the test of time, then it's this one. It was developed during the three-piece rehearsals. Big, loud, fast and complicated, it's built around 'that' bass riff from Squire, but also includes some great work from the rest of the band, with Howe and Downes both shining. Horn – and Downes' vocoder – remind us that this is, indeed, 'Yes'. The song clips along at a speed that almost threatens to run out of control, but it stays together, helped by some arrangement variations – a bouncing guitar section that sounds like it comes from Howe's pen – and a brief, soft section that allows tension to build before the final onslaught. Always terrific live, Horn chose this as the song to perform when he sang with the band on some dates of their 2015 tour, during which the Jon Davidson-fronted band performed the entire album. This was a bold and breathless choice for a 65-year-old, so fair play to him for giving it a go!

The album was released on 18 August 1980 to decent reviews and an expectedly high chart position in the UK of number two, where it managed silver status, although it spent less time on the album chart than *Tormato*. Performance in other territories was less inspiring, however, with the album reaching only number eighteen in the USA. Overall, the album did less well than *Tormato* in all territories, bearing in mind that the 1978 offering itself had hardly set cash registers a-ringing. Most reviewers tended to damn Horn and Downes with faint praise, although the overall progressive tone of the album was noted – this was hardly a complete change in direction.

Until it was rehabilitated after Anderson was removed from the band in 2008, and especially during the full album tours of the mid-2010s, *Drama* has largely been thought of as a 'lost classic'. A great album, forgotten by fans. That's not quite true. For those of us that bought it, absorbed it and loved it at the time, it entered the canon as just another great Yes album. It's in many fans' top fives to this day, and if you are reading this and you haven't heard it, you really need to.

Now it was time to tackle that supposedly-sold out tour. More on that shortly.

Jon and Vangelis – Short Stories

Personnel:
Jon Anderson: all vocals
Vangelis: keyboards, synthesizers, piano, electronics
Raphael Preston: acoustic guitars
Produced By Vangelis
All songs by Vangelis and Jon Anderson
Engineer: Raphael Preston
Mastering: Hitoshi Takiguchi
Recorded: February 1979 at Nemo Studios, London
Released January 1980
Highest chart places: UK: 4, USA: 125

Tracklist: 1. Curious Electric 2. Each and Everyday 3. Bird Song 4. I Hear You Now 5. The Road 6. Far Away in Baagad 7. Love Is 8. One More Time 9. Thunder 10. A Play Within a Play

It is part of Yes folk lore, of course, that Greek musician Vangelis Papathanassiou had tried out for Yes in 1974 when the band were seeking a replacement for Rick Wakeman. However, in the intervening time, the electronica maestro had been building up a solid reputation with a series of albums for RCA. These mixed melodic instrumental pieces – think 'Pulsar' from the album *Albedo 0.39*, for instance – with rather more exploratory compositions such as *Beauborg*. However, these albums sold consistently without giving Vangelis much genuine chart success. His huge fame as a film composer for *Chariots Of Fire* and *Blade Runner* was still ahead of him. What Vangelis did have was a unique vision – a way of looking at composition and creating his sound palette – that nobody had attempted before. His music is instantly recognisable.

The pair had worked together before, when Anderson had provided vocals on the last few minutes of part one of Vangelis' 1975 album *Heaven And Hell*, known on its own as 'So Long Ago, So Clear'. At the end of a lengthy and intense piece of electronic music, Anderson's serene and beautiful contribution provides something of a 'Soon' moment – a few minutes of reflective stillness.

Short Stories came about as a result of four days of improvisation, composition and recording at Vangelis' Nemo studio in Bayswater in London during 1979. How much preparation had been done before the sessions is not clear, but the four days they spent together had the working title Spont (meaning spontaneous) Music, so it's fair to assume not much. It's an interesting, if not completely successful, album. It's at its best when Anderson's contributions surprise, or when he's performing outside his comfort zone, as with the brief but powerful 'Thunder' or the intensity of 'Far Away In Baagad', which sees Anderson's vocals in percussive, almost scat-singing mode. The other strength of the album is, of course, Vangelis himself, who is at his best when mixing his brass-like synth parps with more conventional instruments such as organ, Fender Rhodes and grand piano. The opening piece – 'Curious Electric' – is a thrilling ride through Vangelis' sonic arsenal and has a vocal coda which sees Anderson as a part of a TV set. One thing that Vangelis did always bring out in Anderson was his sense of humour, and here it makes a brief and welcome appearance.

Where the album is less successful, however, is when it either waffles or allows Anderson free rein to overindulge in his sentimental hippie schtick. There are what sound like improvised melodies on pieces like 'Each And Every Day' or 'Love Is' might have been better off with more development rather than hurried onto tape in the name of improvisation. Closing piece 'Play Within A Play' works because Vangelis makes it so, Anderson's contributions are less appealing, and on 'The Road' he resorts to one of his stock devices – Celtic sentimentality.

But *Short Stories* has an ace up its sleeve in the sublime UK hit 'I Hear You Now'. This is the track that gets the balance between Vangelis' swirls and Anderson's crooning just right. It's clear that a lot of work has gone into this piece; Anderson's song is very Burt Bacharach – one of his finest vocal melodies outside Yes – while Vangelis' simple four-note synth scale is an inspired hook. The track won well-deserved airplay, even if it didn't quite chime with the new wave aesthetic of early 1980 and reached the top ten of the UK singles chart – something of an achievement – where it sold to the same crossover audience that had warmed to Yes' UK hit single of two years earlier, 'Wonderous Stories'. The album provided both men with their biggest success to that point, and for Anderson, it was – and remains – his highest charting album outside Yes, peaking at number four in the UK.

If their second album as a duo the following year was to be a more cohesive effort, this set them on the right path, and its success is remarkable.

The duo have rarely played live, but Jon did make an unexpected appearance with Vangelis when the virtuoso keyboardist played a solo show in April 1980, as reported by fan and Yes author David Watkinson:

Jon performed with Vangelis no more than three times and this show was a really special moment for me. A Vangelis solo show has always been a rare occasion anywhere in the world, so to see him play, was a must visit. The show was at the Royal Festival Hall and Vangelis showed his virtuosity as usual; helped by a percussionist and singers, he ran through some fan favourites.

Midway through the show, though, was the unexpected moment that would turn out to be the highlight of the night. Jon Anderson and some of his family were seen in the audience in a central position. In a lull in the performance, some fans, including myself, began to encourage Jon to join Vangelis on stage. Under some pressure, Jon stood up and walked to the stage to a great audience reaction. He went on to sing a few songs together with Vangelis and it was fabulous, as they reproduced very closely what was on the album. The feeling was a joyous one for both the artists and the audience, with a relaxed atmosphere all round.

As quickly as it had started, a giddy audience saw it end, their short duo set going by far too quickly, and then Jon was back seated for the rest of the show. It did, however, make me wonder why they never did a full show together. I haven't found a recording of it, but there does seem that there was a performance in the USA that was recorded and is out there in collector's world.

Rick In Switzerland
What of Rick Wakeman as 1980 got underway?

The year started on something of a high, marrying his second wife Danielle in the Caribbean, who he had met in Montreux. On his return to Switzerland, however, things didn't quite work out as planned. He started a record label – seemingly for Swiss artists – called Moon Records in Montreux and attempted to continue his solo career. He had an album – or at least part of an album – in the can, which was to become *Rock n Roll Prophet*. However, only two tracks were to see the light of day from that material, and they were to be his last recordings for A&M, the organization that had released all his solo work since *The Six Wives Of Henry VIII*.

I'm So Straight I'm A Weirdo' (Wakeman) b/w 'Do You Believe In Fairies' (Wakeman)
Personnel:
Rick Wakeman: keyboards and vocals
Percussion: Gaston Balmer
Backing vocals: Lilianne Lauber
Produced by Rick Wakeman at Mountain Studios, Montreux
Engineered by Dave Richards
A & M Records

'Spider' (Wakeman, Holt) b/w 'Danielle' (Wakeman)
Personnel:
Rick Wakeman: keyboards
Ashley Holt: vocals
Produced by Rick Wakeman
WEA records

The single was 'I'm So Straight I'm A Weirdo', with 'Do You Believe In Fairies', released in February 1980. We all know that Rick has a quirky sense of humour, but these two songs seem to have been deliberately placed to aim at the 'novelty' records market. This is a dangerous game, but with Rick's credibility at an all-time low, he may have felt he had nothing to lose. I bought a copy at the time and there are some positives. First of all, Rick's vocals – yes, he sings both these songs – are passable. You can sort of see the point of the A-side. It's been finely crafted to be a 'hit' (which it wasn't), but its message feels confused. Sonically, the song appears to be aiming for the same territory that The Buggles were inhabiting, but with rather less skill, and if it's a parody of that style, it falls flat. At risk of damning with faint praise, however, it's not hard to admire the craft that went into creating the track in the spirit of a man trying to reinvent himself. If you've never heard it, it's definitely worth a listen, even if it's only once. The B-side, however, is best avoided and one can only imagine that it must have seemed like a good idea at the time. I'm pretty sure I've heard a cover version of this by the late TV comedian John Inman – whose sexuality gave the piece another layer of terrible, infantile humour – but this seems to have been excised from history. Rick's version – complete with chirping 'fairy' voices – is ghastly. When the single failed, A & M refused to release the album. Their relationship was over.

There was another single later in the year, called 'Spider', sung in a pant-splitting falsetto by English Rock Ensemble vocalist Ashley Holt, with a lovely instrumental for Rick's wife, 'Danielle' on the B-side. Produced in a one-off deal with WEA in a limited run of 2000, it again sank with trace. 'Hopefully, one of you has a copy', said Rick at a concert in 1981 before playing the B-side 'because I bought the other 1999.'

In September, he pulled together a new version of his band, The English Rock Ensemble and went on tour, playing medium-sized venues. This version of the Ensemble was to last for a while, and although he was forced to put the band on hold at the end of 1980, its core of Tim Stone on guitar, Steve Barnacle on bass and Tony Fernandez on drums were a very decent unit of musicians. I caught this tour at Guilford Civic Hall in September, and it was a loose affair, with the band combining 'the hits' with some lengthy comedic moments. It was all in good fun, of course, but with a set pushing 150 minutes, it all felt a bit – well – long! The audience was sparse, too. Wakeman, of all people, must have felt disheartened, and his finances were suffering.

A planned supergroup with John Wetton, Carl Palmer and Trevor Rabin was scrapped when Wakeman refused to sign a contract with the Geffen label on principle since the label hadn't heard a note of what they might play. In Wetton's official biography written by Kim Dancha in 2001, the author refers to the singer meeting and playing with Rabin, although it seems not to have gelled at that stage, but for some reason doesn't refer to Wakeman or even Palmer at this stage at all. This is understandable, in a sense, as the deal with Geffen seems to have been brokered by A & R executive John Kalodner, who had recently moved on to the label from Atlantic. Kalodner had taken an interest in Wetton's fortunes for some years, and with Wetton looking to make a complete change in his career – new label, new publishing, new management – this seems to have been the first project mooted for him. Wetton's manager of choice was – surprise, surprise – Brian Lane, and with Wakeman still signed to Lane and at a loose end, it's hardly surprising that his name should be thrown into the ring.

It's also just possible that Rick's heart just wasn't in it, and that the 'stand' over a point of principle was simply a smokescreen to cover his lack of interest. There's no shame in that; after all, Wetton claimed that it was Rick's lack of commitment that scuppered the three-piece band that the pair had put together with Bill Bruford in 1976 (although Bruford blamed Wakeman's label A & M records, who were protective of Wakeman's then successful solo career). Whatever the reasons in late 1980, and putting two and two together, Rick might have ended up in Asia! The discussions over *that* band would conclude with two other Yes men involved, as we shall see.

Jon Anderson – *Song of Seven*

Personnel:
Jon Anderson: lead vocals, acoustic guitar (2), keyboards (1,7,8), harp (9), cover, producer
Ronnie Leahy: keyboards (1-9)
Damian Anderson: keyboards (5)
Ian Bairnson: guitar (1-3, 5-8), bass (2), backing vocals (2)
Clem Clempson: guitar (4,9)
John Giblin: fretless bass (1,3,6-9)
Jack Bruce: bass (4)
Mel: bass (5)
Morris Pert: drums, percussion (1-3, 5-7, 9)

Simon Phillips: drums (4)
Dick Morrissey: saxophone (2,4)
Johnny Dankworth: alto saxophone (3)
Chris Rainbow: backing vocals (2-4, 6,8,9)
Deborah Anderson: harmony vocals (9)
Delmé String Quartet; arranged by David Ogden (9)
Mike Dunne: engineer
All songs by Jon Anderson
7 November 1980 [1]
Recorded: 1980
Released: 7 November 1980
Highest chart places: UK: 38, USA: 138

Following his exit from Yes, Jon signed a solo deal with Virgin records and – taking the label's advance to the South of France – started to work on two musical projects, one each to be on a single side of vinyl. One was about the Russian-French artist Marc Chagall; the other was based on writer Daphne Charteris' book, *A True Fairy Tale*, as Anderson told Dave Roberts of *Prog* magazine in 2016. To date, very little of this music has seen the light of day. To say the label weren't impressed by either project is an understatement, and they asked for their advance back.

A new direction was needed, and Jon found it back in the UK. He re-signed with Atlantic and set to work on tracks, some of which had been demoed or submitted to Yes during the *Tormato* and Paris sessions period. Gathering some of the finest session players in the UK around him, the album took shape quickly. Key collaborators included former Stone The Crows keyboard player Ronnie Leahy and 'backing vocalist for hire' Chris Rainbow, ubiquitous around that time, whose layered vocals are a particular feature on the album. Many of the other players – like Ian Bairnson and John Giblin – were associated with the lighter side of progressive rock.

After his experience with Virgin, Anderson found himself under less pressure to produce hits. He told Sid Smith for *Prog* magazine in 2020:

You know it's funny you make records and then the A & R guy will call you up and say, 'Well John, we just listened to the album and we don't hear a single'. And then that's when I put the phone down. Actually, they thought that 'Some Are Born' was going to be a good one and that there was another one that I felt was pretty good, 'For You For Me'. The opposite of that was 'Take Your Time', which was a lovely, lovely sort of a sweet song.

While the album still has many detractors, particularly for its lightweight songwriting, for me it's rather delightful – a bucolic pleasure if ever there was one, with Anderson's songs beefed up with imaginative – if relatively conventional – arrangements. Some albums have an atmosphere all of their own, and this is one. Just like *Drama*, in fact. It opens strongly with the Vangelis-inspired electronica and drum machine of 'For You, For Me' with Anderson in fine, anthemic, 'proclaiming' mode. Giblin's bass bubbles in a way that Squire's never does, while 'Some Are Born' is more conventional, even poppy, but no less impressive. 'Don't Forget' is less pleasing; a lightweight, if positive, bossa nova. Veteran band leader Johnny Dankworth provides a clarinet solo, and that probably tells you all you need to know. 'Heart Of The Matter' co-written by Leahy, is great fun – with Jon singing about, well, cars and girls. The Jack Bruce Band – also featuring Simon Phillips on drums and Clem Clemson on lead guitar – feature here, while Rainbow provides some trademark backing vocals and Dick Morrisey makes a storming contribution on sax. It's an infectious, fun track and a million miles from Yes. The acoustic, Celtic-tinged 'Hear It' closes the first side.

The first three tracks on side two are where the 'lightweight' criticism usually finds credence, although 'Everybody Loves You' has a certain infectious charm, and Giblin's bass playing again impresses. The languid 'Take Your Time' runs into 'Days', although the song itself, with its Hymn-like arrangement, feels like it might break if you were to blow on it too hard. However, the best is left for last, and the title track is perhaps the finest 'progressive' solo piece by any member of the band *including Olias* and *Fish Out Of Water*. It's stunning and yet fits the gentle tone of the album beautifully, building instrumentally from string quartet to keyboards and massed backing vocals by Rainbow. The main song at its heart is simple, yet the arrangement – with Clemson's guitar outstanding – is exceptional, with no kit drums but Morris Pert's percussion a key feature. Even the most hard-hearted listener's heart will surely melt when Anderson's daughter Deborah shares the final moments with her father. A lost and intensely moving masterpiece? You be the judge.

The album was released in November, to a muted response. Atlantic must have hoped that Anderson's kudos as the former Yes vocalist would give the album the same sort of success at *Drama,* limited though even that was, especially in the light of the success of *Short Stories*, but the album entered the UK chart at a disappointing 38 and lingered for only three weeks. These were different times, even though Anderson's first solo album *Olias Of Sunhillow*, a top ten album in the UK in the long, hot summer of 1976, was only four years old.

A Tale of Two Tours

Yes rehearsed their new show in Lititz, Pennsylvania and began the tour in Canada at the end of August, before journeying through the USA in September and October. There was some nervousness about their reception on the tour since tickets had gone on sale well before the announcement of Anderson and Wakeman's departure. The three performances at Madison Square Gardens early on, with its 20 000 capacity, had sold out. However, it's also clear that despite received wisdom assuming that the whole tour was a big seller, this was not the case. Gregg Praetorius, who promoted the concert at Nassau Coliseum on Long Island, told the author, 'It was in the round, and almost all of the upper deck was empty. We lost our shirts.'

Nonetheless, audiences seemed to receive the new boys well, and with Horn fresh, particularly in the early part of the tour, he handled the older material well enough. However, as the tour began to wear on, Horn – not used to this sort of day-in-day-out performing, and lacking Anderson's stage craft – began to struggle. Unwisely (as admitted by Howe in his autobiography), the existing members had chosen not to adjust the keys of the older material down to suit Horn's voice, which put a strain on him from the get-go.

This should not be overstated, however. A typical set list for the US leg shows only two older pieces in the main set for Horn to wrestle with, 'Yours Is No Disgrace' and 'And You And I'. Although the encores were 'Starship Trooper' and 'Roundabout', audiences tend to be more forgiving of performances for the more exuberant encores. Your author saw the tour on the British leg and remembers Horn being totally fine on the *Drama* material, which made up the bulk of the set beyond the obligatory solo sections. I do remember wincing through 'And You And I', however. The showpiece of that set – during which all the album was played except 'Run Through The Light' – was 'Machine Messiah', which closed the main set.

Two non-album songs were also performed on the tour. 'Fly From Here' had been Horn and Downes' introductory song, and it was played in a form that varied very little from the arrangement when it finally made its way into a Yes album in 2011, as the live version on The *Word Is Live* shows, despite it's rather rough and ready quality. The other song was Howe's 'Go Through This', played more than a tad faster than the version the band had been working on earlier in the year. It's *very* new wave influenced, sounding like Chucky Berry meets Jimi Hendrix meets The Boomtown Rats. Howe mentions in his autobiography that a complete studio version of the song exists and might see the light of day at some point.

After a short break, the band reconvened in the middle of November for a month-long tour of the UK. Amazingly, it was Yes' first full tour of the UK since 1975 – the concerts in 1977 and 1978 being more short-term affairs. These were mainly large theatres and halls since aside from Wembley, which they did not play in 1980, 10 000 seater-plus arenas didn't really exist at that point in the UK.

While, again, this should not be overstated, there was rather more resistance to the new lineup. There were some calls of 'where's Jon Anderson' and 'where's Rick Wakeman', at these shows. In a discussion on the *Yes Music Podcast* in 2020, commentator Geoff Bailie made the point that the relative intimacy of these venues may have been accentuated the effect of this dissent on the two newcomers. Your author attended one of the Hammersmith Odeon shows and remembers sporadic shouting – but nothing disruptive, and it certainly didn't affect the attendance in terms of numbers. Horn discussed the issues he had on the *Yes Classic Artists* documentary:

The problem was, particularly on the songs of his [Jon Anderson's]. They were so high. They are OK when I was in good shape, but with 44 shows with only the old night off, you tend to get worn out, especially when you're not very experienced at it.

In the same documentary, Downes sums it up. 'For Trevor, it was the hardest thing. Because he was stepping into the shoes of the voice of yes.' However, Mike Tait, Yes lighting engineer and tour manager of many years standing, takes a harder line:

There's no way he could live up to what Jon had been doing for the band and to the audience expectation. He was talented in his own way, but it wasn't really Yes. It was a band out there to make money and I don't think it was right at all. It should have stopped. But I guess you gotta make a living.

Super-fan David Watkinson gives his perspective on the *Drama* album and the tour, summing up the devastation that many fans felt:

Unquestionably this choppy waters of the Yes story hit highs and lows in the 80s. My memories of the earth-shattering news of founding member Jon Anderson and Rick Wakeman leaving was, for many, the ending of Yes in the classic decade and for some it was the end the world. In reality, though, with hindsight, it was just yet another blip and fans should have been used to it by then. For myself, I have say I was devastated and for this teenager, who lived Yes, it was as significant as a family death. That seems preposterous now, but I guess my escape in life was Yes.

Of course, I went along with the changes as a loyal fan would do, buoyed by what was a surprisingly good, rocking album in *Drama*. After all, it had the right mixture, a Roger Dean gatefold cover and Eddie Offord back to help produce.

Where Yes caught a cold, however, were with varying performances when they played live in the UK. With a much less forgiving audience, UK fans would not accept anything but musical perfection. They had not heard a poor vocal performance from the band in ten years. Additionally, Jon Anderson was more than the voice of Yes, bringing his personality, that 'special something' that being the founder of the band brings.

Looking back though now, who would have thought that this moment for Yes fans would not be as crucial as many initially thought. There would many more changes. 'Perpetual Change', you could say.

But there's a humorous sting in the tail. Chris Squire spoke about Trevor Horn in the *Yesyears* documentary from 1991:

To this day, now he's one of the most successful producers in the world, whenever I see him, he still says. 'You know I have this recurring nightmare, that I'm in a limo with you on the way to Madison Square Garden. You get out a Walkman, and you say, 'Trevor, listen to this tape. You've never heard it before, but if you check it out, I reckon we can play it tonight.'

Ironically, Jon Anderson was also crisscrossing the UK at exactly the same time as his former band. Indeed, someone shouting 'where's Jon

Anderson' at a Yes show might well have received the perfectly reasonable answer 'he's here in two weeks time'. Anderson's solo tour had a slightly different profile – he played more one-night stands in theatres, rather than sometimes performing more than one night in the same venue as Yes did. Also, Anderson's one London show was at the Royal Albert Hall – the home of many a Yes show in the past and future but not in 1980 – whereas his old band played six London shows on the trot at three different venues. It's also clear that these solo shows were considerably less well attended than the Yes concerts. Again, the author attended the show at Birmingham Odeon on December 4, and remembers that it was half full. It's also possible (though not corroborated at the time of writing) that some of the shows were cancelled.

Controversially, despite what I consider to be an excellent show by Yes (despite Horn's voice issues), the Anderson show is more fondly remembered by me. This may be due to the availability of two excellent bootlegs of the tour, which still get regular plays, from Sheffield and London.

However, perhaps it was the freshness of the set which impressed most. It was built largely around *Song Of Seven*, but also *Short Stories*, and Anderson's large – and presumably expensive – 'New Life' band featured many of the musicians that had appeared on the album, including Morris Pert, Chris Rainbow, Ronnie Leahy, Dick Morrisey and John Giblin, while session drummer Barry D'Souza and guitarists Jo Partridge and Les Davidson stepped in to complete the lineup. Claire Hamill supported the band with a short acoustic set.

The breadth of this band gave Anderson plenty of arrangement options to play with, and he took full advantage. Not only did they play an excellent arrangement of themes from Stravinsky's ballet *Petruschka* midway through the set, but the band's thirty minute Yes medley – played early in the performance – remains the boldest re-imagining of Yes material attempted by any member of the band during their solo careers. It's certainly worth finding on YouTube if you haven't heard it, but unusual tracks thrown into the mix included sections of 'To Be Over', 'The Prophet', 'Rejoice' (heavy on the reggae), plus the holy trinity of 'The Revealing Science Of God', 'The Remembering' and 'Ritual' from *Tales From Topographic Oceans*.

The main set closed serenely with 'Song Of Seven', and at The Royal Albert Hall, Anderson's daughter Deborah reprised her role from the album. At other shows, Chris Rainbow's falsetto did the job. Forty years on, Anderson still views the band he put together for the tour with great affection, telling Sid Smith in *Prog* magazine in 2020:

> I found over the years that if you get the right bunch of people together in a band that's in harmony with what you want to do, it's like sailing a boat. It's so easy. I've only done it maybe four or five times in my career where I get together five or six people, and you can sense that they want to really engage.

It was in the rehearsals for the tour that Anderson's talent as a musical director – albeit one with a relatively rudimentary knowledge of music theory – really came to the fore. The band were rehearsing a jam that would take place in the middle of the set that would give Anderson a short break. The singer spotted that there was a lack of direction in what the band were playing. He told Sid Smith:

> I said to Ronnie Leahy, that he could learn the three main melody lines from *Petrushka* by Stravinsky. He was like, 'okay Jon'. I was really unsure, but they did it.

The results – as anyone that has heard the live recordings from the show will testify – were stunning.

Both tours ended a week or so before Christmas 1980. As well as the inevitable performance anxiety, touring with Yes in the autumn and early winter of 1980 also gave Trevor Horn an insight into the ramshackle way that the band's finances were handled. 'During the whole year I earned 10 000 dollars', he told Chris Welch, 'and that was given to me in cash on a plane.' He was not given all the wages he should have had for the tour as the money had run out. He also refused to sign a document telling him that he 'owned' 20% of the production budget – his share requiring him to pay $25 000. Horn's cause was helped by the business acumen of his wife, Jill Sinclair, who by this point was a part-owner of SARM West studios. Jill (who died in 2014 after an eight-year struggle with her health) is usually credited with Horn's move into production, although it's no surprise that Brian Lane also lays claim to this. Horn remembers a conversation between Jill and Brian Lane in which she berated the Yes manager for his financial trickery. In short, it seems that the financial complexities that had – partially at least – led to the departure of Anderson earlier in the year were far from at an end. What next for everyone?

Yesshows

Personnel:
Jon Anderson: lead vocals, guitar, keyboards
Steve Howe: electric and acoustic guitars, backing vocals
Chris Squire: bass guitar, backing vocals, percussion on 'Ritual'
Patrick Moraz: keyboards on 'The Gates of Delirium' and 'Ritual'
Rick Wakeman: keyboards on all other tracks
Alan White: drums, percussion
Chris Squire: production, mixing
Mike Dunne: live recording
Nigel Luby: live recording engineer
Geoff Young: engineer
Tony Wilson: production on 'Don't Kill the Whale'
Roger Dean: cover painting
Recorded 1976 to 1978 at various locations
Released: November 1980
Highest chart places: UK: 22, USA: 43
Tracklisting: 1. Parallels 2. Time and a Word 3. Going for the One 4. The Gates of Delirium 5. Don't Kill the Whale 6. Ritual (Part 1) 7. Ritual (Part 2) 8. Wonderous Stories

But after all the activity that had taken place over a crazy year, there was one last sting in the tail. *Yesshows* – a two-LP set and the band's second live album – was released in the USA and the UK in the autumn. It was very odd timing. During some downtime in the summer of 1979, Squire holed up at home and mixed tracks for a selection of Yes concerts during 1976 (with Patrick Moraz in the band) and 1977 and 1978, on the *Going For The One* and *Tormato* tours. The 1979 version of the band had reviewed the material and sat on it. Squire's mixes were considered to be for reference only, and there was a move to make it a triple album to mirror *Yessongs*.

From a fan's point of view, it's a slightly uneasy mix of the good, the bad and the ugly. On the plus side, the Roger Dean cover is delightful – one of his best in this author's opinion – and the track selection is interesting, although a little rigid in its 'no repeated tracks that are on *Yessongs*' policy. As a result, it's a rather unbalanced mishmash of material and fails to achieve what the best live albums do, (and which *Yessongs* did), which is to make you feel that you're at an actual concert by the band. One of the main issues that Howe, Anderson and Wakeman – and Anderson, Moraz and Wakeman knew nothing about it until it was released – had with the record was that some of the edits were unsympathetic and unrealistic. The main example of this was the sudden edit between 'Time and A Word' (recorded by the BBC at Wembley in 1978) and 'Going For The One' recorded the year before, when in fact the 1978 set had seen a fast jump into 'Long Distance Runaround' at that point.

However, if the main purpose was to represent some of the band's longer pieces, then it did a decent job, with an incendiary performance of 'The Gates Of Delirium' and a very fine – if lengthy – 'Ritual' (albeit padded out by a pointless introductory jam, with Anderson's spoken thankyou's). Ironically, repeating songs from other live albums has been much less of an issue in the 21st century, when live albums by the band have been coming thick and fast.

In the end, however, it has been perceived by the band (except Squire and to a lesser extent White) as a cash-in exercise by Atlantic, and if the Horn / Downes version of the band had any hope of continuing, then the release of this celebration of the second half of the 1970s can hardly have helped the fragile band's confidence.

1981 - Telephone Secrets

The Split

In early January 1981 (according to Steve Howe in this autobiography), the five members of Yes met at the Howe residence in Hampstead to discuss the future of the band. As a result of this meeting, the band ceased to exist for the first – as so far, only – time in its life. In the 21st Century, the word 'hiatus' is frequently used to mask band breakups. But the early 1980s were a different time, and the band had ceased to be. There was no going back. For the next two and a half years, there would be no Yes.

Again, Brian Lane has a different perspective, telling Daryl Easlea of *Prog*:

> At the post-mortem meeting, the band decided that it was my fault their tour had not succeeded and by mutual agreement, I quit, having suggested to them that to re-energise the band, they needed to go round to Jon Anderson's house and when he opened the door, throw themselves at his feet and beg him to come back.

While all of this is disputed, it does seem that Steve Howe and Geoff Downes were left holding the baby. Squire and White made it clear that they were forming a band with Jimmy Page of Led Zeppelin while Trevor Horn – whose tenure was always likely to be a short one, considering the trauma of the British tour – decided to carry on with the next Buggles album, and then moved, famously, into production. We'll track his progress through 1981, and as he sweeps in and out of the Yes story, but in the main, we'll leave his production career for another book. It's certainly worth it. Meanwhile, Howe and Downes had to decide what to do with Yes – and in the end, made the decision that replacing three members was too much of a stretch. For now, this was the end.

To read Brian Lane's testimony, you would believe that all of a sudden, he had lost two bands – The Buggles and Yes. But it also appears that he hung around in managing all but Horn, at least for a while. But what of Squire and White?

XYZ

One thing that has always puzzled me is why Chris Squire was so keen to jump ship, given his herculean efforts to keep the band together during 1980. As the date of the Yes meeting was in early January and the final date of the UK tour had been December 18, plans for Squire and White to join Page clearly came together very quickly, with White saying that he met Page for the first time at a Christmas party (1980 being the implication). But Squire must have known that the band would probably not continue with that line-up. Squire is vague about this on the *Yes Classic Artists* documentary admitting that a chequered tour wasn't in itself a reason to split, then giving an excuse about Horn moving into production. This doesn't quite ring true, so it's likely that his and White's exit, while not preplanned necessarily, came about because they felt the project with Page might be more promising.

Some context is also required to the liaison that was to become called XYZ (ex-Yes and Zeppelin). John Bonham, Zeppelin's drummer, died on 24 September 1980 and it wasn't until December 4 that the band put out a press release saying that they had formally called it a day. By all accounts, Page was a broken man at this point, and for him to start another project so soon after the demise of the band cannot have been easy for him.

Yet attempt to do so, he did. What happened next is often glossed over by Led Zeppelin commentators. Chris Salewicz, in his so-called *Definitive Biography* of Page – which devotes less than a fifth of the book to the last 40 years of Page's career – tosses off XYZ in one short paragraph and in doing so badly misrepresents this time. A much better – indeed fascinating – account of the fledgeling band's fortunes comes in Martin Power's *No Quarter: The Three Lives Of Jimmy Page*. Power reports that Page and Squire – who both lived in the Surrey area at the time – first met at a party and discussed the idea of forming a band together over Christmas 1980.

Initially, it seems that Squire had simply lost interest in music as reported by keyboard player Dave Lawson in an interview in 2015, in Power's book: '…he was floundering a bit. [He] was only getting up at three in the afternoon. Basically, he'd lost interest.' Nonetheless, Squire soon regained his enthusiasm as he, Lawson and Alan White started to work up material together, with the help of the new-fangled Synclavier keyboard. Page did not fully come on board until February 1981, by which time a fair amount of material had already been written. Robert Plant was also supposed to be involved, but as Squire later told *Guitar World:* 'Robert never showed.' Various reasons have been given for this – from the thinking (as Alan White has suggested) that the proggy nature of the material was too complex for Plant, to Squire's assertion that it was down to 'feelings between Robert and Jimmy'. It was just too soon for them both. There has even been a suggestion that John Paul Jones was to be involved on keyboards, and while there's a logic to this, it still seems far-fetched.

Four demos from the sessions are available to listen to on YouTube and have been poured over by both Yes and Zeppelin fans for many years to discover clues as to how this group might have sounded. In truth, not too much should be read into what we have available to us, in the same way that far too much time has been spent overanalysing the recordings from the Paris sessions at the end of 1979. Including by your humble author.

An instrumental track that was later to become the very decent 'Fortune Hunter' from the second album by Page's 1980's band The Firm shows a fair amount of promise, as does the one piece from the demos, the catchy, Squire sung 'Telephone Secrets', which is offered in a rough but reasonably developed form, with layered backing vocals. It's the most frustrating piece on offer here, as it's never seen the light of day in any other form – and it's great! When news broke that in 2013 that the band were working on a new album – tragically, Squire's last – there were strong rumours in the Yes fan community that this track was to be dusted off and that it would appear on the album that became *Heaven and Earth*. It didn't, and now it's presumably too late.

There's also an instrumental based around the riff that later became 'Mind Drive' from *Keys To Ascension 2,* although this is repetitive and underdeveloped, while the demos also offer up the first recorded version of 'Can You Imagine?' (here called 'Can You Believe It'), later to appear delightfully on *Magnification*, also sung by Squire.

The interesting question is if Lawson was so involved, where are the keyboards in the demos, except for the piano on 'Can You Believe It', which may just as well be played by Squire or White?

As for the future of the band, Lawson does give a somewhat speculative and possibly metaphorical account – laced with a good dose of humour – of a summit meeting between the managers for the two camps, Brian Lane and Peter Grant, also reported in Power's book:

I think the respective managers landed in their separate helicopters. Kick-off commenced, the conversation lasted about five minutes and then they returned to their various helicopters and left.

While it's likely that one of the reasons that XYZ didn't continue derives from a lack of agreement between two strong-minded managers – and how often have we heard *that* – it also seems that Page, who, according to Squire had been on a health kick following Bonham's death, began to slip back into his bad habits. Although one is tempted to say 'pot/kettle' to Squire, given his own tendencies in the 1980s, Page's 'issues' do seem to have blighted his life on a day to day basis far more than Squire's. Whatever the reasons, the sessions fell apart in the spring.

'Run With The Fox' (Squire / White / Sinfield) b/w 'The Return Of The Fox' (Squire / White)

There is a coda to the story, however, and there was to be one release from Squire and White at the end of the year. 'Run With The Fox' was an unashamed attempt to tap into the lucrative Christmas singles market, especially (but by no means exclusively) in the UK. The song features lyrical contributions from Peter Sinfield, whose work on Greg Lake's 'I Believe In Father Christmas' – a massive hit and a Christmas 'classic' – was well known and was considered commercially expedient. Also involved were some old friends and relations – Andrew Pryce Jackman, who provided orchestrations; the St.Paul's cathedral choir, led by Squire's old choirmaster Barry Rose; Dave Lawson on keyboards and Squire's then-wife Nikki on backing vocals.

Much beloved of Yes fans, 'Run With The Fox' is simply terrific. While its chances of making the top ten anywhere were obviously remote, and it did indeed sink without trace, it is both a terrific song and a great example of the Great British Christmas Single. Whereas 'I Believe In Father Christmas' derived its hook from 'Troika' by Sergei Prokofiev, here it's the 'Sussex Carol', a traditional English tune passed down the generations and first notated by Ralph Vaughn Williams in 1919. Recorded by the ever-present (at the time) Nigel Luby, Squire and White produced.

Had the song been recorded by Yes in (say) 1975, it might have been a big hit. As it is, neither Christmas songs nor ex-members of bloated prog bands were in any way 'cool' in 1981. But both Squire and White provide excellent performances, with Squire providing lead vocals and also his most prominent bass work since *Fish Out Of Water*. It's wonderful stuff, and worth seeking out either online, on the *Yesyears* box set or indeed on *Chris Squire's Swiss Choir* released in 2007.

'Return Of The Fox' is essentially an instrumental version of the A-side and very much a 'play it once' affair.

Rick Wakeman – *1984*

Personnel:
Rick Wakeman: keyboards, production, composer
Steve Barnacle: bass guitar
Tim Stone: guitar
Tony Fernandez: drums
Gary Barnacle: saxophone
Frank Ricotti: drums
Chaka Khan: vocals
Kenny Lynch: vocals
Steve Harley: vocals
Tim Rice: vocals, lyrics
Jon Anderson: vocals
Recorded: 23 February–14 April 1981, Morgan Studios, London
Highest chart positions: UK: 24
Track listing: 1. 1984 Overture a) Part One b) Part Two c) War Games 2. Julia 3.
Hymn 4. The Room (brainwash) 5. Robot Man 6. Sorry 7. No Name 8. Forgotten
Memories 9. Proles 10. 1984

Rick Wakeman – *The Burning* (Original Soundtrack)

Personnel (Wakeman tracks only):
Rick Wakeman: keyboards, composer, production
Alan Brawer: guitars, production
Kevin Kelly: bass
Mike Braun: drums
Recorded and mixed at the Workshoppe Recording Studios, New York, 1980.
Tracklisting: Wakeman Variations: 1. Theme From The Burning 2. The Chase Continues
3. Variations on the Fire 4. Shear Terror and More. Music From The Film: 5. The Burning
(End Title Theme) 7. The Fire 10. The Chase 11. Shear Terror (other tracks not shown)

In early 1981, things began to look up for Rick. He signed to M.A.M – a
huge entertainment agency where he was looked after by Tony MacArthur.
MacArthur managed to get Rick a multi-album deal with Charisma –
seemingly a good fit, considering that label's pedigree for working with
progressive artists. Furthermore, Rick's first album with the label was to
be a (relatively) big-budget adaptation of the George Orwell novel *1984*
with lyrics by Tim Rice (*Jesus Christ Superstar*, *Evita* and *Chess*) and a
host of guest stars, including soul diva Chaka Khan, Steve Harley, Jon
Anderson, comedian Kenny Lynch and Rice himself.

On the face of it, this seemed like a good move. Not unlike the 500th anniversary of the arrival of Columbus in the Americas in 1492, the early 80s saw a glut of projects built around the build-up to this famous date. An instrumental album by former Genesis guitarist Anthony Phillips, released in the same month as Rick's album, was given the same name, and a movie of the book, which was eventually to star John Hurt and Richard Burton, was also in development.

The website *openculture.com* described the album thus in 2017:

The perfectionistic Wakeman himself looks back on his *1984* with embarrassment. 'In retrospect, a mistake,' he has said. 'The wrong album at the wrong time, with all the wrong people around at the time.... I formed the wrong band, (the worst I have ever had), the deal for the stage show fell through and all in all, I listen back to the music with my head in my hands.' Luckily, we are not bound to respect an artist's assessment of his work. Wakeman's music and Rice's lyrics take the leaden, grey world of Winston Smith and Julia and turn it into a carnival, moving from soaring ballads to rockers with the sneering vaudevillian satire of *The Rocky Horror Picture Show*.

Despite Wakeman's misgivings, there's little doubt that *1984* marks something of a return to form. Recorded from February to April 1981 at Morgan Studies in London, the material is, on the whole, strong and varied, and the performances are good, although Chaka Khan feels a touch out of place on her songs, which also represent the main showcase tracks on the album. The record was given a big enough budget to feature a choir and an orchestra, though both feel somewhat superfluous, here, as if they exist because, well, Rick *always* has those things, doesn't he? But in terms of melodies, playing and production, the album is hard to fault within the context of Rick's solo output. It's very decent indeed.

While the vocals by the guests beyond Khan are all somewhat mannered – one thinks of both Harley and Rice in this respect – Anderson gives a fine and committed vocal performance, and many of the instrumentals are very fine indeed. That said, Rick's keyboard choices are somewhat suspect, with a greater reliance on the then-innovative but less sonically distinctive Prophet 5 and 10 analogue polysynths. However, the themes and arrangements are, in the main, excellent and had the album been released in the mid-70s, we might now be hailing it as a classic. Instead, it's considered an embarrassment by its creator, which is grossly unfair.

The album reached a very creditable 24 in the UK. Hardly comparable with Rick's mid-1970s heyday, of course, but considering how unfashionable he was at the time, something of a triumph. Sadly, a planned spin-off musical version was scuppered when the producers were unable to get permission from George Orwell's estate to use the material on the stage.

1984 was not the only album released by Wakeman in 1981, with Charisma also giving a release to his soundtrack album *The Burning*, which had been recorded in 1980. While the album itself isn't of the standard or budget of *1984*, with not all of the music by Rick at all, some of his melodies have stood the test of time well, and the main theme was played on the *1984* tour in a medley that also included 'Anne Boleyn'.

Rick took the album on tour in the autumn of 1981. The band was largely the same as the one that had toured the year before and had played on the album, but poor old Ashley Holt was inevitably replaced by a female vocalist, who was mainly there to sing Chaka Khan and Jon Anderson's (!) parts. British singer and one-time member of jazz vocal combo Wall Street Crash, Cori Josias got the job, making a decent (if occasionally pitch-challenged) fist of the *1984* material, and also some of the inevitable vocal pieces from albums like *Journey*. I saw the tour at Hanley Victoria Hall, and I remember that while Ashley Holt was missed, Ms Josias was a pleasing replacement for this nineteen-year-old Wakeman fan. The live footage and recordings from the tour also demonstrate how good Rick's then-band were – both Tim Stone (guitar) and Steve Barnacle (bass) were excellent players, and by this point, the band were extremely tight. As a result, one suspects that Rick's less than favourable view of his band may be influenced by his unhappy memories of the time overall.

Jon and Vangelis – *The Friends Of Mr. Cairo*

Personnel:
Jon Anderson: vocals, composer
Vangelis: composer, producer, arranger, performer
Dick Morrissey: saxophone, flute
David Coker: voices
Sally Grace: voices
Dennis Clarke: saxophone
Claire Hamill: backing vocals
Carol Kenyon: backing vocals
Roger Roche, Raine Shine: engineer

Recorded at Davout Studios, Paris, and Nemo Studios, London, 1981
Highest chart placings: UK: 6, USA: 64
Tracklisting: First issue: 1. The Friends of Mr Cairo 2. Back to School 3. Outside of
This (Inside of That) 4. State of Independence 5. Beside 6. The Mayflower
Second issue: 1. I'll Find My Way Home 2. State of Independence 3. Beside 4. The
Mayflower 5. The Friends of Mr Cairo 6. Back to School 7. Outside of This (Inside of
That)

With *Short Stories* something of a success, Polydor understandably wanted
a follow up from Jon and Vangelis swiftly, and they got one in fairly short
order, with the release of *The Friends Of Mr. Cairo* in July 1981. If *Short
Stories* had felt like a Vangelis album with a touch of added Anderson in
various places, then the follow up saw Anderson asserting his character
rather more on the writing, while Vangelis experimented with some
slightly more conventional and rhythmic arrangements.

Anderson learnt a lot during his time making the first two albums with
Vangelis, particularly considering their relatively short recording periods.
In 2020 he told Sid Smith of *Prog* magazine about the need to write words
at a quick pace:

I was learning how to be spontaneous lyrically. Watching him [Vangelis]
work taught me so much musically speaking. I remember he was
recording in Paris, what was going to be *The Friends of Mr Cairo*. He was
actually playing a groove as I happened to walk in and I sang 'State of
Independence' – the whole thing, spontaneously without thinking. The
whole shape of the song in one long take.

There are, of course, two versions of the album; the first with its stylish
Art Deco white cover that was released in July 1981, and the rerelease
from January 1982, which has a larger cover photograph and contains the
hit single 'I'll Find My Way Home' (of which more in a moment). While
sequencing on an album isn't always important, here it is. The sequencing
on the 'white' album is almost perfect, with the lengthy title track – very
much the centrepiece of the album – up first, whereas the rerelease opens
with the big hit and relegates 'Friends' to side two. In doing so, the whole
vibe of the album is altered in a negative way. It may have made the album
more commercially successful but unbalanced it as a 'listen'.

So, we'll take a quick look at the album as it was originally sequenced.
I remember hearing the title track for the first time at the time of release

and was delighted. As a lover of many of the same films as Jon (through the influence of my father), this tribute to the movies of the 1930s and 1940s was very evocative, including as it does impersonations of many of the stars of that era by British voice actors David Coker and Sally Grace. The title is a reference to Peter Lorre's character in *The Maltese Falcon* and both he and Sidney Greenstreet, as well as Humphrey Bogart, are impersonated. This 'gimmick' did not please everyone, but to these ears, it just about falls on the right side of the 'cool v cheese' divide. Vangelis bubbles away rhythmically, with both bass synth and piano prominent. The track itself goes through three distinct phases: the initial verses, with voice actors and that exotic melody; then the more intense 'Father love...' section, with its more abstract, Yes-like lyrics and then a complete change for the final half of the piece, a more expressive and romantic end to the track. On balance, the piece does benefit from the voice interjections since they cleverly set up each of the sections. Overall, this title track is something of a masterpiece – quite possibly Jon and Vangelis' most impressive twelve minutes.

You've never heard Vangelis play like he does on 'Back to School'. It's a 1950s pastiche that is not to be taken too seriously, but it felt as tiresome then as it does now, despite a splendid rock and roll sax solo, falling on the wrong side of that same 'cool v cheese' divide. 'Outside Of This (Inside Of That)' returns to the slightly surreal torch songs that populated *Short Stories* but does it pretty well, held together by a lush keyboard arrangement.

Side two kicks off with 'State of Independence', with Vangelis once again offering up a very rhythmic keyboard and percussion arrangement (including handclaps throughout the song) and one of Anderson's chant-along vocal melodies. Whether by luck or judgement, the end result is terrific, bolstered by some tremendous sax playing again. This version – at almost eight minutes – is probably two or three minutes too long, but nonetheless, if Anderson can make a claim to have written a 'standard' in his 50-year career, then this is it. Donna Summer had a top twenty hit in the UK with the song the following year, and Moodswings had a minor hit with it in the early 1990s with guest vocalist Chrissie Hynde, calling it 'Spiritual High'. Anderson is well aware of the song's power, returning to it himself in 1994 for his superb *Change We Must* solo album and playing it regularly in his solo shows.

The ballad 'Beside' is more direct than most Jon and Vangelis ballads, although the Greek musician's electric grand piano, rather than his trademark synths, is probably the only sound on the album to have dated badly. The album closes on another 'high concept' piece, with the charming and atmospheric 'The Mayflower' charting the journey of those early American settlers, comparing it with a speculative sci-fi voyage by a spaceship called 'The Mayflower'. Shades of *Olias*, perhaps? It's another delight – the two musicians combining beautifully, with Vangelis delivering an expansive synth arrangement.

Jon and Vangelis – 'I'll Find My Way Home' (Anderson / Vangelis)

Released initially as a stand-alone single at the end of 1981, backed with 'Back to School', this is much less adventurous and far poppier than anything on *Friends Of My Cairo*, with a very basic arrangement from Vangelis. As a result, it feels incredibly lightweight, though the synth arrangement does hint at the Greek musician's main theme for *Heaven and Hell*, which had also been a minor success in the singles charts in 1981, alongside his iconic theme from *Chariots Of Fire*. Given that Vangelis was never so popular and commercialy successful before and after, it's hardly a surprise that this simple song should perform much better in the race for the Christmas number one slot than Squire and White's far more satisfying offering released at the same time, reaching the heady heights of number six. Nor is it really a Christmas song, although its theme of 'homecoming' is one that is very associated with the yuletide period.

The rerelease of *Friends Of Mr. Cairo* in January 1982 also outperformed the initial release, reaching number six in the UK, compared to its relatively lowly seventeen in July 1981.

The Buggles – *Adventures In Modern Recording*
Personnel:
Geoff Downes: keyboards, drum programming, production (tracks 3, 4 and 7)
Trevor Horn: vocals, bass, guitar, drum programming, production
John Sinclair: drum programming, cymbals, guitar, vocals, production
Simon Darlow: keyboards and guitar
Chris Squire: sound effects (tracks 1 and 9)
Anne Dudley: keyboards
Luís Jardim: percussion
Bruce Woolley: vocals

Danny Schogger, Rod Thompson: keyboards
Gary Langan, Julian Mendelsohn: engineering
Recorded Sarm East Studios, London, 1981
1. Adventures in Modern Recording (Darlow/Horn/Woolley) 2. Beatnik (Horn) 3.
Vermillion Sands (Downes/Horn) 4. I Am a Camera (Downes/Horn) 5. On TV (Horn/
Wooley/Rodney Thompson) 6. Inner City (Darlow/Horn) 7. Lenny (Downes/Horn) 8.
Rainbow Warrior (Darlow/Horn/Sinclair) 9. Adventures in Modern Recording (reprise)
(Darlow/Horn/Woolley)

Trevor Horn was at something of a crossroads, though he might not have
realised it at the start of 1981.

Initially, the plan had been for Horn and Downes to start work on
another Buggles album, but by the spring of 1981, Downes had moved on
to Asia, leaving Horn to record the album on his own, although Downes
actually co-wrote and co-produced three of the songs on the album,
'Lenny', 'Vermillion Sands' and the song that they ended up offering
to Yes for the *Drama* album, 'I Am A Camera'. Unfortunately, Downes
departure, while seemingly amicable, led to unforeseen consequences,
with Island records dropping Horn, believing the project to be at an end.
Adventures In Modern Recording, when it finally appeared, was released
on the independent Carrere, a French label best known at the time for
Euro pop and for some commercial success with heavy rock band Saxon.

Sometimes viewed as a white elephant of an album considering its lack
of commercial success in the UK, *Adventures In Modern Recording* is an
exceptionally interesting record on several levels. However, despite being
very diverse, it hasn't dated well due to its booming drum machine and
early 1980s synth textures. It also, as Horn himself was at pains to point
out towards the end of the project himself, lacks an obvious hit single.
There is no shortage of catchy melodies, but these are often buried in
off the wall arrangements that leave the listener slightly off-kilter rather
than charmed. Here we hear Horn flexing his muscles as a producer as
much as a songwriter, so there are quirky touches all over the album, and
the overall vibe is very much of any anything goes, thrown-everything-
including-the-kitchen sink at it, approach. It's art pop of the most
mannered but intriguing kind. Imagine early 80s Thomas Dolby without
such great songs, or the Godley and Crème 10CC tracks. I dare you.

Take, for instance, the title track which opens the album and satirises
modern musicians – it's catchy and the album's most obvious single, yet
it's an unsettling listen, while 'Beatnik' combines a plodding rockabilly

arrangement with Beatles harmonies. It's not hard to imagine a Yes arrangement of 'Vermillion Sands' (with lyrics that draw on Horn's love of the writings of J.G. Ballard) despite its bubbling bassline, which borders on the progressive, and Downes' huge synth fanfares also hint at Yes. Indeed rumours persist that Horn had already drawn up plans for a follow up to *Drama* called *Vermillion Sands,* so the progressive nature of this track is hardly surprising. The final minute or so offers up a Glen Miller pastiche, presumably to sum up the decadent vibe of Ballard's Sci-fi resort.

Lovers of *Drama*, and 'Into The Lens' will find it hard to listen to 'I Am A Camera' without the Steve Howe soloing, but it's interesting to hear how little the song itself was changed for the extended Yes version, though the Buggles 'take' emphasizes the Bert Bacharach nature of sections of the melody. 'On TV' was another single and might have made an off the wall hit with a bit of luck, while 'Inner City' continues the synth pop direction. The album finishes strongly and in art rock style with 'Lenny' (about Leonardo da Vinci). It is the final Horn / Downes composition and was a top 10 hit in Holland. The stately 'Rainbow Warrior' is another track that might have welcomed a Yes arrangement before a final burst of the title track completes the main album.

While not added until a 2010 reissue, the demos of the track that introduced Downes and Horn to Yes 'We Can Fly From Here' can be heard, as well as two other pieces that appeared on the 2011 Yes album *Fly From Here.*

We will leave Horn to his own devices for a year or so shortly, although it's important to understand the shift in his stature as a producer during the time between the end of the *Drama* tour and his employment as producer on *90125* late in 1982.

Adventures was released in November 1981, and sporadic promotional appearances took place, finishing with an appearance on Dutch TV in April 1982. By the time that the album had been released, Horn had already started working with British pop duo Dollar. The duo – David Van Day and Thereze Bazar – had already placed themselves squarely in the Saturday-morning children's TV market with a slew of UK hits during 1978 and 1979, but 1980 had seen their success dry up. However, under Horn's direction, they had a sequence of four top twenty hits written by Horn and his cohorts Bruce Wooleey and Simon Darlow – Downes was not involved by this point. All four songs feature lush, inventive Horn arrangements and production, and while 'Give Me Back My Heart' and 'Hand Held In Black And White' both had bubblegum melodies, albeit

Above: Rick and band take their bows at the end of the *1984* show at Hammersmith Odeon in 1981. (*David Watkinson Collection*)

Below: Tony Kaye and Trevor Rabin with Cinema in 1982. (*David Watkinson Collection*)

with sophisticated arrangements and Bazar's trademark breathy vocals, both the biggest hit 'Mirror Mirror' and the final one in the Summer of 1982, 'Videotheque', which features a bold key change before it's chorus, might easily have been viable Buggles songs. Indeed, a demo of 'Videotheque' can also be found on the 2010 reissue of *Adventures*.

By the time that Horn was approached to be involved in the Cinema project that morphed into Yes, he was a hot property due to his inventive production job on the equally stylish ABC's *Lexicon Of Love* album. Dollar gave him hits, but ABC cemented his reputation as a producer. This lead to the purchase of Basing Street Studios from Chris Blackwell of Island, renamed SARM East. Work with Malcolm McLaren, The Art Of Noise, Propaganda and Frankie Goes To Hollywood was to follow. And, of course, Yes.

1982 – A Tale of Two Supergroups

Asia – *Asia*

Personnel:
John Wetton: bass, lead vocals
Steve Howe: guitars, backing vocals
Geoff Downes: keyboards, backing vocals
Carl Palmer: drums, percussion
Released: 18 March 1982
Recorded: Marcus Recording (London, UK) and Town House (London, UK) June-November 1981
Producer: Mike Stone
Engineer: Mike Stone
Cover Illustration: Roger Dean
Highest chart position: UK: 11, US: 1 (9 weeks)
Tracklisting: 1. Heat of the Moment (Wetton/Downes) 2. Only Time Will Tell (Wetton/Downes) 3. Sole Survivor (Wetton/Downes) 4. One Step Closer (Wetton/Howe) 5. Time Again (Downes/Howe/Palmer/ Wetton) 6. Wildest Dreams (Wetton/Downes)7. Without You (Wetton/Howe) 8. Cutting It Fine (Wetton/Downes/Howe) 9. Here Comes the Feeling (Wetton/Howe)

At about that same time that XYZ was beginning to get serious, the band that Kalodner had been trying to pull together with John Wetton finally began to take shape with the bassist teaming up with a now-available Steve Howe. The pair got together, found common ground and began pooling material for an album. Howe gave his impressions of Wetton on the *Yes Classic Artists* documentary:

> Brian [Lane] called me and said 'I've met John Wetton. He's not doing anything'. So, we went into Redan Studios and we just played together for a couple of days. And I thought boy, this is great. What a singer. What a bass player. Nothing like Chris; not a thematic bass player. Such a climber; builder. And I thought that was the kind of group we're going to make. A sort of high-end musical group, like Yes started out to be, with lots of technical prowess going on.

The group needed a drummer. According to Wetton's biographer Kim Dancha, one of the names in the ring was Alan White, who – unsurprisingly – never showed up to play. But the band's first choice was Simon Phillips, who rehearsed with Wetton and Howe at Redan and seemed keen to take part, although in the end, it came to nothing, although Howe remembers Phillip's short time with the band fondly. Wetton (via Dancha) doesn't mention Phillips at all but DOES mention White.

In the end, it was Carl Palmer that got the nod. The former ELP drummer had recently formed his own band PM, playing short, new wave-influenced pop rock material, but the band had been largely ignored. So, come mid-1981, Palmer was available. Again, he gelled with Wetton and Howe, so a three piece was formed. With (according to Howe in his autobiography) Wetton and Palmer looking to keep the band as a power trio, it was Howe who felt that the group needed a further dimension, and so Geoff Downes was invited to take part. Wetton said, in his official biography:

Geoff was really an unknown quantity to me, but I saw a great deal of potential in his approach to the keyboard, which was less of a virtuoso but more into the textures and quite modern sounds with computers, and his writing. I thought this was actually a very good way for us to go.

The auditions didn't stop there, with Howe recalling that onetime Journey vocalist Robert Fleischman and Trevor Rabin (again?) invited to audition as a fifth member, with Brian Lane not sure that the band were strong enough with Wetton singing lead. Did they need another guitarist? Did the band need a vocalist? Even hitmaker Roy Wood was involved at one point. In the end, though, the band decided to stay as a four-piece. It was a good decision.

Much of the criticism that Asia received when their debut was released in 1982 derives from a feeling that their chosen music was created to appeal to the highest number of people possible, rather than from artistic endeavour. There's some truth in this. The presence of a major label at an early stage certainly bears this out, and there's also little doubt that the 'progressive' leanings of Howe and Palmer were toned down to suit a wider audience. What is also clear, however, is that Wetton's own leanings were in the direction of shorter songs anyway, as evidenced by his excellent – and largely unsung – 1979 solo album *Caught In The Crossfire*. Downes was a prog fan, but his work with The Buggles had demonstrated that his real talent was in tone and texture. He was ideal for Asia, whereas it might be argued that Howe – and perhaps even Palmer – weren't.

In the end, part of the reason that Howe's initial tenure in Asia didn't last as long as it might have, is that the planned writing partnership between the guitarist and John Wetton didn't really gel, and it was, instead, the partnership of Wetton and Downes that was to become the big money-spinner.

There's also little doubt, however, that the resulting debut really worked, chiming in directly with what American audiences (in particular) were looking for in 1982. Part of this is down to Mike Stone's expert production, which – while reverb-heavy – balanced the instrumental prowess of the band against the quality of the songwriting and the harmonies. There's an epic feel to much of the music – especially on side two – even though no track gets close to reaching six minutes, and Stone's production is both distinctive and timeless, unlike much of the music that came out of the 1980s.

One area in which Stone's production does succeed admirably is in getting the best from Wetton's voice. While he was never a great singer technically, he did have a lot of warmth in his singing (when it was at its best) which Stone brings out despite the epic feel of the music. Crucially, the 'Englishness' of some of the playing simply comes across as 'unusual'. Stone's most recent production had been *Escape* by Journey, an excellent – indeed iconic – album, but one in which the performing had been relatively conventional – very much in the American style. One wonders if most pop/rock fans had heard anyone play quite like Steve Howe or Geoff Downes unless they had heard a Yes album. But this was a different demographic. The music must have felt familiar yet other-worldly at the same time.

The album benefited hugely from the extended rehearsal period through the middle of 1981 before recoding started formally, allowing the band to refine its arrangements, which are concise yet bold, enhancing the songs rather than detracting from them. No other album – not even one by Asia – sounds quite like this. It's commercial, but in a very unusual way, and It *really* works.

The album starts with a bang, and the massive hit single 'Heat of The Moment', yet even this is not quite as conventional an arrangement as it sounds on first listen, and Howe's extended solo is not what most listeners might have expected. There's not a whammy bar in sight! 'Only Time Will Tell' (another hit in the USA) keeps the tone quite light, but the album hits top gear with the fabulous 'Soul Survivor', perhaps the band's best amalgamation of the talents of all four musicians. It rocks hard and the moments of tension and release are expertly crafted. Oh, and the

Moog scale from Downes is delicious, Wakeman fans! It's a great song, made better by a fantastic arrangement. Note also Palmer's double bass drum work just before the fade.

We enter 80s pop territory with the relatively unsung 'On Step Closer'. This is a Howe co-write and the listener can almost smell his writing in the verses particularly – it sounds like it might have ended up on the GTR album four years later had it not been for Downes' distinctly 80s keyboard tones, but it also provides Howe's most expansive and inventive moments on the album. 'Time Again' progs up, giving Palmer the room for some more expansive playing, before settling into another catchy rocker with a prog/jazz twist and some great piano moments, not to mention an inventive vocal arrangement. It's another reason that the album worked so well and ends side one in great style.

Side two contains only four tracks, allowing a touch more room for instrumental expansion. 'Wildest Dreams' also has some proggy moments, built around another catchy Wetton-inspired song, and has a drum solo, of sorts. 'Without You' is the 'big ballad' – it's nicely done, with some great moments from Howe, but sniffs of some of the latter Yes's more turgid moments. In short, it's more of the same, but at a slower tempo. By 'Cutting It Fine', the formula is well established. If the album has a fault (and it doesn't have many) it's that it's occasionally a bit same-y in terms of the song writing and tone, with the Asia 'stomp' once again in evidence. That said, there are plenty of instrumental variations on display, particularly a great acoustic guitar intro and a lovely piano-and-synth-based end section, which is as good as anything on *Drama*. The final piece is a tour de force and the perfect closer, a track that Wetton had been working on since well before the band's formation. 'Here Comes the Feeling', despite another 'stomping' but catchy chorus, really allows the band to express itself with the rigidly defined areas of its strong structure. Only the guitar-based instrumental section (after the terrific synth solo) lets the track down a bit – it's a little weak. But overall, it's a great climax.

Over the years, I've occasionally considered whether Steve Howe was the 'right' guitarist for Asia. After he left, the band had a succession of more conventional rock guitarists, like Pat Thrall and Mandy Meyer. These musicians usually played Howe's parts well (as Trevor Rabin has always done in Yes) but when asked to come up with their own, tended to make more conventional choices, to the detriment of the music in terms of distinctiveness, at least. One of the reason's that the first lineup of Asia was such a success was because of the unconventional nature of the

Right: A very rare photograph of a very relaxed Cinema – captured in mid-1982 at John Henry Rehearsal Studios, London. Left to right: Trevor Rabin, Tony Kaye, Alan White, Chris Squire. (*David Watkinson Collection*)

Left: The Buggles – Geoff Downes and Trevor Horn – pre Yes, circa 1979.

Right: ABWH in 1989. Left to right: Jon Anderson, Steve Howe, Bill Bruford, Rick Wakeman.

Gary Lilley,
6 Gibbons Walk,
Biddick Hall Estate,
South Shields,
Tyne & Wear.

28th May 1980

Dear Gary,

I don't think we have written to each other before but having read your letter and card the other day at the office, on behalf of Chris, Alan and myself this personal reply many console you a little.

The group is not over although your kingpin, Jon Anderson, has departed. There are so many reasons why we want and must continue the group and when you have heard the new album I feel confident that you will sympathise with this desire. Often Jon has proclaimed his own importance in the group and at times has overemphasised his own importance and hidden some of the contributions made by the rest of us. The continuation of Yes will put a more accurate definition on everyone's endeavours of the last 12 years.

Now you will get a clearer idea of what Jon wants to do via his own records, likewise with Rick, and the rest of us reformed into a solid unit will carve a new niche for Yes.

Regards,

Steve Howe

P.S. Of course, good luck to Rick & Jon

Directors: S. J. Howe, Mrs J. M. Howe, O. A. Be...
Vat No: 240 2176 06 Registered Co No: 1080386 Registered Of...

This page: There was much upset over the departure of Jon and Rick in 1980. However, in this pre-internet age, you could write to a member of Yes and get a personal reply, as these letters from Steve Howe and Alan White show.
(*David Watkinson Collection*)

---

yes music ltd

9 Hillgate Street, London W8. 01-727 2791/2/3/4 Telex 25728

Gary Lilley,
6, Gibbons Walk,
Biddick Hall Estate,
South Shields,
Tyne & Wear.

27th May 1980

Dear Gary,

Just a note to let you know that I am also sad about what has happened in 'YES', but LIFE must go on. The new music we are creating is such a rebirth, that I have not been so enthusiastic about 'YES'music for a few years.

Knowing your dedication to the band for so many years, I thought a personal note was maybe in order.

Yours in music,

Alan White

Directors: J. R. Anderson S. J. Howe C. R. E. Squire A White O. A. Beuselinck
Registered offices: 23 Albemarle Street, London W1X 4DB
Registered company no: 701157   VAT no: 240-0084-21

This page: *The Age of Plastic* – the hit debut from The Buggles, released in 1980. Despite the bubblegum pop of 'Video Killed the Radio Star', there are plenty of positive hints at what the band could offer Yes. *(Island)*

Left: The Yuggles? Yeggles? Or just…Yes? A promo shot from 1980. (*David Watkinson Collection*)

Right: Roger Dean's cover for *Drama*. It's almost unique in his output for Yes, in that it combines his normal style with a striking, contemporary 1980s aesthetic. (*Atlantic / Rhino*)

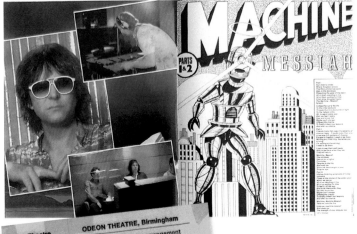

Left: Two pages from the *Drama* tour programme, featuring band shots – including Alan White playing the marimba – and Peter Hills' strikingly kitsch artwork for 'Machine Messiah'. (*David Watkinson Collection*)

Left: A ticket for a Yes show on the Drama tour in Birmingham. It would have set you back £4 – a pound less than seeing the band at Wembley two years previously. (*David Watkinson Collection*)

Below: *Yesshows* – an oddity released in 1980, showcasing the Wakeman / Moraz lineups, and released without Moraz, Wakeman or Anderson knowing about its release. (*Atlantic / Rhino*)

Above: A guess pass for Madison Square Gardens earlier on the same tour.

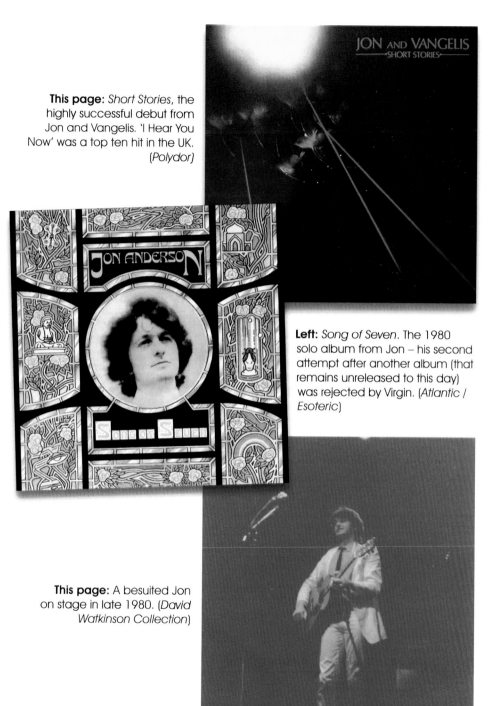

This page: *Short Stories*, the highly successful debut from Jon and Vangelis. 'I Hear You Now' was a top ten hit in the UK. (*Polydor*)

Left: *Song of Seven*. The 1980 solo album from Jon – his second attempt after another album (that remains unreleased to this day) was rejected by Virgin. (*Atlantic / Esoteric*)

This page: A besuited Jon on stage in late 1980. (*David Watkinson Collection*)

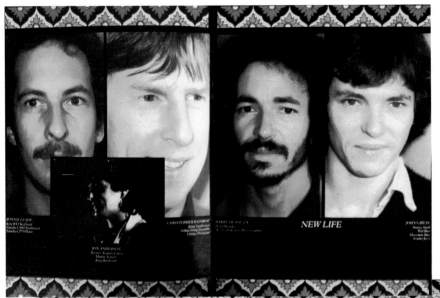

REHEARSALS

Above: Two pages from the Jon Anderson 'Tour of the 1980s' programme from 1980. The photographs show what an amazing band he built around himself – the cream of British session players. (*David Watkinson Collection*)

Right: A ticket from the same tour. Seeing the band (supported by Claire Hamill) in Glasgow would have cost you £5. (*David Watkinson Collection*)

Right: *1984*, Rick's big-budget comeback for Charisma in 1981, with lyrics by Tim Rice. It's a mixed album in terms of quality and considered embarrassing by the artist, but I like it! *(Charisma)*

Left and below: Two shots from Rick's 1981 tour. The three backing vocalists were only there for the Hammersmith show, but Cori Josias handled the lead vocals well and Rick's band were excellent. (*David Watkinson Collection*)

Left: The Buggles – *Adventures In Modern Recording*. Largely a Trevor Horn solo record, this experimental album saw him playing with production techniques in art-pop style. (*Carrere*)

Right: Jon and Vangelis – *The Friends of Mr Cairo*. This is the cover for the original (and better sequenced) pressing, prior to the hit single 'I'll Find My Way Home' being added to later versions. (*Polydor*)

Left: Chris Squire and Alan White closed 1981 with 'Run with the Fox', a fabulous and little-known Christmas single with lyrics by Peter Sinfield. (*Atlantic*)

Right: *Animation* – Jon's third solo album, and another cracker, with a harder, more electronic tone than *Short Stories*. It featured an army of keyboard players, including David Sancious and Dave Lawson. (*Polydor*)

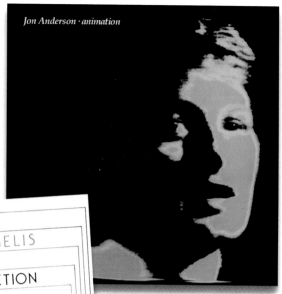

Jon Anderson · animation

Left: Jon And Vangelis – *Private Collection*. To some, a symphonic masterpiece; to others, a snoozefest. (*Polydor*)

Right: Phil Carson. In 1982, Carson was an executive at Atlantic, and was instrumental in linking Trevor Rabin with Squire and White, as well as tempting Tony Kaye back into the world of Yes. His importance in the story of Yes in the 1980s cannot be overstated.

Left: Cinema rehearse at John Henry Rehearsal Studio in London in mid-1982. Alan White – note the electronic components of his kit – is here pictured with a concentrating Chris Squire. (*David Watkinson Collection*)

Right: The Hammond-man – Tony Kaye - rehearses with Cinema in 1982. (*David Watkinson Collection*)

Left: Having been to his wedding a few weeks previously, Jon Dee shows Alan White photos of the drummer's nuptials, while sound man Nigel Luby looks on. (*David Watkinson Collection*)

Right: A smiling Alan White rehearses with Cinema in 1982. (*David Watkinson Collection*)

Left: A youthful Trevor Rabin and Alan White rehearsing in 1982. (*David Watkinson Collection*)

Right: Trevor Rabin and Tony Kaye at John Henry rehearsal studios in London, 1982. (*David Watkinson Collection*)

Above: A good view of the two-level Asia stage set up in London in 1982. (*David Watkinson Collection*)

Below left: John Wetton with Asia in London in 1982. (*David Watkinson Collection*)

Below right: A smiling (and semi-naked) Carl Palmer takes the audience applause with Asia in London in 1982. (*David Watkinson Collection*)

Right: *Asia* by Asia. The debut album is an almost unique combination of pop tunes, prog instrumentation and state of the art 1980s production. (*Geffen*)

Left: *Alpha*. Was there ever such a fall from grace? It represents the perfect example of a record company misunderstanding what made an album successful in the first place. The result is a near-disaster. (*Geffen*)

Right: With Wetton out of the band temporarily, Greg Lake stepped in for a few shows in Japan, and did a great job. The shows were also to be Steve Howe's final ones with the band.

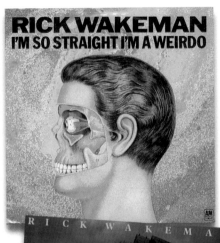

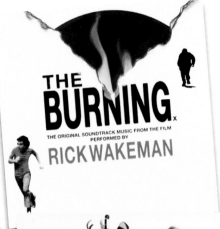

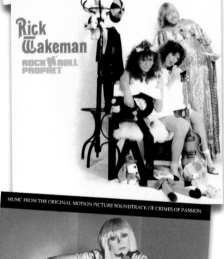

This page: Rick Wakeman from 1980 to 1984. Rick struggled to find an audience during this period. The bold but flawed 'I'm So Straight I'm a Wierdo' single was his last for A & M, and there were three decent movie soundtracks plus two patchy but not completely unsuccessful rock albums. (*A & M, Moon, Charisma*)

Right: *90125.* A huge hit all over the world. It placed Yes back on or near the top of the album charts – even in the UK, where the band were about as uncool as it is possible to be. *(Atco / Rhino)*

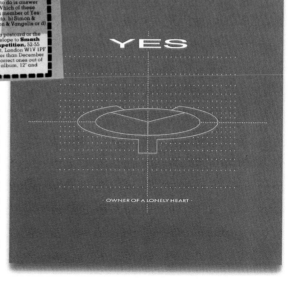

EX-POMP ROCKERS IN "WE LIKE LONG SONGS" SHOCK!

"It would be a shame if we were written off as a has-been band," says Jon Anderson, singer with **Yes.** "We've grown up with and pushed the current electronic boom and now we want to give off a new vibe of the modern musical age."

"Yes were formed in 1968 and for years were the leaders of 'techno-flash' or 'techno-rock' — pompous stuff with lots of painful soloing. At the end of the decade, while every punk worth his safety pins was listing Yes along with ELP and Genesis as The Band To Hate, the individual members all drifted into making terribly indulgent solo LPs.

For a while Jon Anderson was replaced by the two members of Buggles — Trevor Horn and Geoff Downes — but now they're back in a near-original line-up with Trevor Horn producing instead of singing. The result is the radically different single (and current *Smash Hits* office turntable fave) "Owner Of A Lonely Heart".

There's an LP too, called "90125" after its catalogue number because the six members couldn't agree on any other title. Making the record was the first time Jon had met his successor, Horn.

"He was great. I tried to get him to sing on the album but he wouldn't. Don't worry, I'll drag him on stage when we play London."

Under Horn's influence, the old Yes excess (they used to do 45-minute songs) has been "squeezed down".

Live, they plan to extend it again. "I want to captivate people," says Jon, "so they totally escape . . . like in a film. That's why I prefer long songs, they're more of a challenge."

And talking of challenges, here comes one of those tricky *Bitz* competitions. The prize is a copy of "90125", a 12" of "Owner Of A Lonely Heart" and a truly bonzer Yes poster.

All you have to do is answer this question. Which of these duos features a member of Yes: a) Rene & Renato, b) Simon & Garfunkel, c) Jon & Vangelis or d) Tik & Tok?

Answers on a postcard or the back of an envelope to **Smash Hits Yes Competition**, 52-55 Carnaby Street, London W1V 1PF to arrive no later than December 7. The first 15 correct ones out of the bag get an album, 12" and poster each.

Left: So successful were Yes in 1983 that they even found their way into uber-trendy pop rag *Smash Hits.* *(David Watkinson Collection)*

Right: 'Owner of a Lonely Heart'. The band's number one smash hit in the USA, and massive worldwide. It was a real team effort. The basic song was by Rabin; Squire and Horn tweaked it; Anderson sprinkled some lyrical fairy dust over it and provided an iconic lead vocal, while White played the famous Fairlight horn stabs. *(Atco)*

Above: Part of David Watkinson's 1980s Yes memorabilia display, taking in the periods 1980 to 1982. (*David Watkinson Collection*)

Right: David Watkinson with Chris Squire at the Cinema rehearsal in London in 1982.

Left: David Watkinson outside the London Yes offices in the early 1980s with Jon Dee and fellow Yes fan Dougie Craig. (*David Watkinson Collection*)

playing and the arrangements, combined with the rather more familiar nature of the songwriting. As I've mentioned, if the album has a fault, it is that the core songwriting is a little one-paced on a couple of songs, leaving the arrangements to pick up the slack. But it's a remarkable piece of work. We have not seen its like since.

Some (but not all) of the reviews were savage. The oft-quoted Robert Christgau of *Village Voice*, said this:

> The art-rock Foreigner is a find – rare that a big new group is bad enough to sink your teeth into anymore. John Wetton and Steve Howe added excitement to contexts as pretentious as King Crimson and Yes, but this is just pompous – schlock in the grand manner, with synthesizers John Williams would love. And after listening to two lyrics about why they like their girlfriends, three about 'surviving,' and four about why they don't like their girlfriends, I'm ready for brain salad surgery. Inspirational Verse: 'So many lines/You've heard them all/A lie in every one/From men who never understand your personality.'

This is cruel, but – as is often the case – not without an element of truth. However, people – especially Americans – *liked* the schlock, and with some help from the likes of Godley and Crème to produce state-of-the-art videos for the brand-new MTV, the band began a period of almost unimaginable commercial success.

Looking back at it now, it seems almost impossible to imagine that two bands made up of crusty old members of 1970s 'dinosaur' groups should have such success over the course of less than two years. However, Asia tapped perfectly into the zeitgeist. Almost by coincidence (although not without a little commercial intent), this music was exactly what audiences were looking for in the spring (and indeed summer and autumn) of 1982. The album spent an astonishing nine weeks in the number one spot in the *Billboard* Hot 100. Both 'Heat of The Moment' and 'Only Time Will Tell' were top twenty hit singles in the USA (at a time when that meant something). Elsewhere, the album performed well but not spectacularly, although 'Heat of The Moment' was also a top ten hit in Germany. A Grammy nomination also followed.

The band took to the road across the summer and autumn of 1982. The evidence suggests that in the USA they started out in theatres and pretty much stayed in them. However, they toured long and hard in the USA, returning to areas where shows had sold out months before. When the tour moved to other countries, the band generally played fewer dates in larger venues (including Wembley Arena in London, in October 1982). The band played the whole album, plus early arrangements of some tracks that would appear on *Alpha*, like 'Midnight Sun' and 'The Smile Has Left Your Eyes', plus solo spots for all four members.

Despite its undoubted quality, to this day, it's an album that continues to split the crowd, generally treated with cautious 'thumbs up' within the progressive rock community. Forty years later, however, reviews on *Progarchives* still throw up words like 'crap' and 'terrible', with their ire generally focussed on Wetton for dumbing down his prog credibility with fame and fortune in mind. This is simply not the case. Any artist is allowed to take his music wherever his muse takes him, and while there's no doubt that the lucrative contract with Geffen required some commercial intent, the first Asia album is an almost unique blend of progressive rock chops and Wetton's natural tendency (evidenced as early as 'Book Of Saturday' from King Crimson's *Larks Tongue In Aspic)* towards writing melodic pop-rock songs.

However, after huge – some might argue almost unnatural - commercial success, surely the only way for Asia was down.

Jon Anderson – *Animation*

Personnel:
Jon Anderson: vocals, acoustic guitar, production, composition
Clem Clempson: guitars
Stefano Cerri: electric bass guitar
Chris Rainbow: vocals
David Sancious: keyboards
Simon Phillips: drums and percussion
Dave Lawson: keyboards
Ronnie Leahy: keyboards
Blue Weaver: keyboards
Delmay String Quartet: strings
Billy Kristian: guitar
John Giblin: bass guitar
Jack Bruce: bass guitar
Ian Wallace: drums
Brother James: percussion
Morris Pert: percussion
Brazil Idiots: Brazilian percussion

Neil Kernon: producer
Tony Visconti: producer, 'All God's Children'
Recorded 1981-1982
Highest chart positions: UK: 43, USA: 176
Tracklisting: 1. Olympia 2. Animation 3. Surrender 4. All in a Matter of Time 5.
Unlearning (The Dividing Line) 6. Boundaries 7. Pressure Point 8. Much Better
Reason 9. All Gods Children (Jon and Jennifer Anderson)

Undaunted by any perceived lack of success of the *Song Of Seven* project, Jon began compiling material for this next solo album at the start of 1981. There was to be a change in record company in the UK, with Polydor set to release the next album, although Atlantic would still release it in other territories. It's clear that Jon still had not used up his kudos from his success with Vangelis. There was a decent recording budget, and Polydor put a fair amount of effort into promotion. Your author remembers seeing adverts for *Animation* on the London tube in April 1982.

Tony Visconti was initially approached to produce the album, as Jon recalls in the sleeve notes to the Esoteric reissue of the album, but in the end, freelancer Neil Kernon came in to co-produce. Jon suggests that he might have come from a recommendation. Just a likely, he was a record company appointment, although Visconti did come in for one day, producing the exuberant but undemanding album closer 'All Gods (sic) Children', which Jon had written with his wife Jennifer in a mild panic on learning that the in-demand producer was available for just one day.

The band assembled for the album was out of the top drawer. Clem Clempson's lead guitar was retained from *Song Of Seven*, as was the 'one man choir' that was Chris Rainbow. Rainbow suggested bassist Stefano Cerri (one of the bubble-y finger-style players so fashionable at the time), while on drums came the ubiquitous Simon Phillips and the astonishingly-talented David Sancious – there for his keyboard skills but equally adept on guitar. Other guests included several of the *Song of Seven* musicians Ronnie Leahy, Morris Pert, John Giblin and Jack Bruce (who played fretless bass on a couple of cuts), plus a crossover with the XYZ band via keyboard player Dave Lawson, who overdubbed on six songs on July 30 1981, and was paid a very decent £517.50 for his pains, Lawson reports. John's old bandmate in The Warriors, drummer Ian Wallace, also made a brief appearance.

Sonically, Jon seemed to have got his 1979-80 'folk phase' out of his system. *Animation* – while it's not completely successful – is nonetheless quite a triumph. Certainly, the influence of Vangelis is there, both in the increased evidence of electronica and also in some of the vocal arrangements. As Jon told Malcolm Dome in the notes for the 2021 Esoteric reissue:

> From my point of view, introducing this electronic approach into what I did made sense. I was creating music in a world that had previously been shut off to me because I was a little intimidated by what technology had to offer. But on the album, I opened up my horizons and took the first steps down the path on this remarkable journey. What I discovered was a taste for artistic adventure, and that's something which is remained firmly with me to this day.

Infact, despite the early 80s polysynths and the then-fashionable Yamaha electric grand (now a dated sound outside the latest Keane album), the album has something of a timeless quality that makes it very listenable today. Clempson's lead guitar work is first-rate, as is Phillip's hard-hitting drumming. This is an album with a much tougher rock edge, as evidenced on opener 'Olympia', which celebrates the technological revolution, and has drumming as hard as anything produced by Alan White. The nine-minute title track mixes a progressive structure (not unlike a harder-edged 'Song of Seven') with some cloyingly direct and sentimental lyrics, but it is terrific despite that. 'Surrender' is the attempt at a hit single – a light-as-a-feather cod-reggae with a children's chorus. It's a bit nasty, but over quickly, while the equally short 'All In A Matter Of Time' is, by contrast, a little wonder – uplifting and infectious, with a terrific synth solo from Sancious.

Both 'Unlearning' and 'Pressure Point' on side two continue the hard edge, with strong rhythmic textures to the fore, albeit with the emphasis of electronic and programmed percussion. However, sandwiched between them is the Celtic-tinged 'Boundaries'. The same melody was to appear twice more, once on the Yes album *Open Your Eyes* and also on the Jon solo album *The Promise Ring*. In the *Animation* reissue, Jon claims the reuse of this melody to be coincidence. Personally, I doubt that – but there's no shame in reusing your own tune once in a while, even if it does sound like it was written in Scotland in the 1700s.

Prior to the Visconti-produced closer, 'Much Better Reason' sets a jazzier tone, but is also of high quality, while the reissue also contains the exuberant but messy 'Spider', the B-side to 'Surrender' and a demo-quality version (provided by Jon on cassette) of 'The Spell' – a lengthy, impressionistic tone poem recorded during the *Animation* sessions but vetoed by the record company.

The album was released in June 1982, and despite some promotional heft, did less well in the UK than *Song of Seven*, peaking at 43 and a horrific 176 in the USA (although a number three placing in the Netherlands can't be sneezed at). The core band – with Guy Shiffman depping for an unavailable Simon Phillips – played a series of dates across the summer of 1982 in the USA. Recordings of the tour – which never extended beyond North America – are of excellent quality but are far more Yes-orientated than the 1980 UK jaunt, with the band making a decent fist of a much less adventurous series of Yes medleys. Why did the tour not continue? Jon puts this down to a lack of managerial impetus. It's certainly true that around this time, Jon's personal manager was shared with Vangelis, so it's understandable that Jon's solo career might not have been top of the priority list. It's also understandable that Jon might decide that after another commercial failure – for now – perhaps his career might be best off allied to his eccentric Greek partner in crime. Indeed, Jon even suggests that his touring ambitions were stymied by his reintegration into Yes, although on this score – given that those events were to come almost a year later – he is perhaps misremembering.

Nonetheless, *Animation* stands up as a worthy and adventurous solo album, and one of Jon's finest.

The Birth of Cinema

So, at the start of 1982, with XYZ now a distant memory, Squire and White were still looking for another project. They did jam a little with Phil Lynott of Thin Lizzy, originating a track that was to become 'Don't Talk About Me Baby', the final (and, it has to be said, pretty awful) track from Lynott's second solo album *The Phil Lynott Album*.

Phil Carson, then a senior vice-president at Atlantic, now enters the picture as the main catalyst for what was to happen next. Also, at this point, Trevor Rabin, who we've already discussed in relation to his brief flirtation with John Wetton as a possible member of (what was to become) Asia now re-enters the picture.

Born in South Africa in 1954, Rabin had been a 'whizz kid' session guitarist in his native land before forming teen-pop sensations Rabbitt. That band (with Rabin singing) became the biggest group in South Africa in the mid-1970s. It should be pointed out at this point, that while the band shared the same sort of success in their homeland that the likes of The Bay City Rollers were enjoying in the UK, Rabbitt were no uber-hyped, manipulated teen band. The standard of songwriting was strong, and Rabin produced their debut album *Boys Will be Boys* himself, with not a session player or label Svengali in sight. They even debuted with a successful cover version of Jethro Tull's 'Locomotive Breath'.

Later years had seen a solo album from Rabin (on which he played everything except drums) followed by a move to London, and two further solo albums for Chrysalis, *Face to Face* and *Wolf*. Both were inventive and well-produced albums in the hard rock style that have stood the test of time. However, although much-hyped around 1979 and 1980, while the New Wave Of British Heavy Metal (a movement that Rabin was only on the fringes of) was burning at its brightest, he had won only a cult following. He even toured the UK in 1979, supporting former Gong progressive artist Steve Hillage – an odd pairing, in retrospect.

Following the lack of success of *Wolf*, by 1981, Rabin had moved to Los Angeles to try his luck, armed to the teeth with demo tapes. It was Rabin's former mentor, Zimbabwean Robert John 'Mutt' Lange that pointed Rabin in the direction of Phil Carson. Lange and Carson were colleagues due to the fact that Lange had produced several albums (including the massive seller *Back In Black*) by AC/DC for Atlantic and the band were part of Carson's stable. It is through such associations that great bands are born. And probably some terrible ones, too. Anyway...

Now aware of, and impressed by Trevor Rabin, Carson suggested the South African to Squire and White. Rabin flew into London in early 1982, met with Squire and White in a Chinese restaurant in Shepherd's Bush (according to White on the *Yes Classic Artists* DVD), followed by a terrible – probably slightly drunken – jam back at New Pipers, Squire's house in Virginia Water. 'The worst jam ever,' said Squire. Nonetheless, the trio got along. A new band was born. They named it Cinema.

Next up was a keyboard player. Accounts differ slightly here, but it's likely that the initial impetus to recruit Tony Kaye came from Carson. As he said on the *Yes Classic Artists* documentary:

I said to them [Squire and White], 'let's go and get Tony Kaye back'. They said to me, 'but he hasn't been in the band for ten years'. I said 'he was the original keyboard player, guys. Let's get him back'. Tony had a certain magic as a live player. He had a great image; he looked good up there; he added something.

Squire – who himself sometimes claimed credit for Kaye's recruitment – saw the benefit of having a player with a simpler style in the band. Kaye flew in, and rehearsals began at the voluminous John Henry space in Brewery Road in the Islington part of London. While Rabin's initial involvement had seen him working on some of the material that Squire and White had been rehearsing with Jimmy Page, they also began integrating some of the songs that Rabin had been touting around into rehearsals.

At around the middle of the rehearsal period, Jon Dee, who at the time was the editor of *Yes Music Magazine*, visited the band at the rehearsal space with David Watkinson. The two discussed their visit in detail with Kevin Mulryne and Mark Anthony K of the *Yes Music Podcast* in February 2020. It provides a fascinating insight into the progress that the new band had made to that point. Jon Dee explains how the two of them became some of the only people to see the Cinema band play live:

Chris Squire was the person that invited me down there. I was talking to him and Alan White a lot on the phone at the time. Nigel Luby [the band's sound technician] was a friend who lived quite close to me in Earls Court, so I arranged the date with him. Nigel made us welcome and got us a cup of tea. Infact, I'd just been to Alan White's wedding reception, so in a way that made things more relaxed was because I had the photographs from that which Alan was keen to see, so that was a nice ice breaker. The guys were playing on a slightly raised platform, and they were very keen for us to walk amongst them. It was quite a strange experience. First of all, it was really loud and the music sounded really powerful and so energetic. It was a Yes fan's ultimate dream.

They started with a song called 'Carry On', followed by 'Make It Easy' and then a really interesting song called 'Open Your Doors', which had Chris on lead vocals. In between each song, Tony Kaye was basically rehearsing the intro to 'Hearts'. It was interesting hearing Tony's keyboard style, with his rhythm-based playing and his great Hammond technique.

David comments on the vibe in the room:

It was all very chilled. We had to walk past other bands rehearsing to get to the band – I remember we walked past Gary Moore – but when we arrived, there was a general air of relaxation, particularly from Chris. Then it went from 1 to 100 when the music started and there was so much energy. It was shockingly good, and we didn't really expect how good Trevor would be. As a unit, they were already really tight.

Jon then discussed the set that they played in a bit more detail:

One of the questions that Dave and I had before we went in, was how close to Yes will this be? Or will it be more like Asia? I was hoping that there would still be an element of Yes, but when we heard the music, we were reassured. The other question was, what would Trevor Rabin be like? We now know that his technique is very different [to Steve Howe] but at the time, we had no knowledge as to how he would fit in. But he was just amazingly powerful. 'Carry On' was amazingly powerful. Tony Kaye had quite a simple set-up; he had an OBX [an early Oberheim analogue polysynth], two Hammonds and an electric piano [actually a Yamaha electric grand, rather than a Rhodes or Wurlitzer].

Then they went into 'Make It Easy', which is know to Yes fans as the live intro to 'Owner Of A Lonely Heart', although [the complete song] has now been officially released in various formats. I was amazed at how fast he could play, and I remember thinking that if ever these guys played Yes tracks, he'd have no problem playing the Steve Howe parts. I have to say that what we heard in the rehearsal studio was ten times better than the final recorded version.

Finally, the last complete song they played had Chris Squire on lead vocals; the first two songs had been sung by Trevor Rabin. 'Open Your Doors' had Alan White playing Simmons drums for the whole thing. It was really interesting and might have fitted onto *90125*.

However, it was clear even at that stage that the band needed a lead singer. In the interview with Kevin and Mark, David Watkinson speculated that he didn't think the band could have carried on as a four-piece and been really successful and that they needed 'that distinctive voice', although Jon Dee disagreed with that view. In the end, well into the recording process (1983 and many months after Jon and David witnessed the rehearsal) that the decision was made to bring in another singer.

Given that the instigator of the line-up was Carson, it was only natural that he should take the package to Atlantic and approached Doug Morris – then President of the US side of the label – with the idea. Morris put up a (relatively paltry) $150 000 for development and recording, which

Carson later supplemented with $150 000 of his own cash. It's clear that Trevor Horn's participation as producer was part of the 'selling' process, as he was now 'hot' after the huge success of ABC's pop-soul classic *The Lexicon of Love* in the early part of 1982. Indeed, Squire had asked Horn to be lead vocalist with the project, and – according to Jon Dee – he was mightily tempted to be part of it, even attending a few rehearsals in 1982. However, wiser heads prevailed, and Rabin and Squire went into the project as lead vocalists with Horn producing. Those than knew him thought he was mad to jump into bed with such 'dinosaurs'. As Horn says himself on the *Yes Classic Artists* documentary: 'I was doing really well. And everyone thought I was mad to go and do Yes.'

But by the autumn of 1982, the material had been developed to the extent that the band could move into the studio with Horn, where they were to remain for eight long months. In the interview with Jon Dee and David Watkinson on the *Yes Music Podcast*, the question arose as to whether there was still Cinema material that had yet to seen the light of day. We know that neither 'Carry On' or 'Open Your Doors' made the final track selection for the album. Other pieces were no doubt being rehearsed; there's no suggestion that the three songs played on that day were all that the band had in their locker at the time.

Infact, in 1982 the only name on the lips of the band as a potential producer was Bob Ezrin – the American producer who had worked with Pink Floyd on *The Wall* and remains active today. Horn seemed to have pulled back from the project having decided not to sing. Trevor Rabin told *Rock Candy* magazine at the end of 2020 that two other names in the frame were his old mentor from South Africa, Mutt Lange and also Roy Thomas Baker. He recalls having dinner with them both at the same time in London, and that they got along famously. Another intriguing development was that the band were initially to be called not Cinema, but Ice. But both names, as it turned out, were used by other bands. Indeed, when word got out that a band signed to a major label were called Cinema, all the other bands with that name issued lawsuits. 'Funny how they sued us and not each other', commented Rabin, ruefully.

Rick Wakeman – *Rock n Roll Prophet*

Personnel:
Rick Wakeman: keyboards, vocals, composing, production
Lilianne Lauber: backing vocals
Gaston Balmer: percussion

Dave Richards: engineering
Recorded at Mountain Studios, Montreux in 1979
Released 1982
1. I'm So Straight I'm a Weirdo 2. The Dragon 3. Dark 4. Maybe '80 5. Early Warning 6. Spy of 55 7. Do You Believe in Fairies? 8. Rock 'n' Roll Prophet

Rick's private life continued to challenge him in 1982, with a new partner in model and singer Nina Carter after the failure of his marriage to Danielle and some attempts at rebuilding his finances following a move back to the UK from Switzerland. As a result, there was only one release from him in 1982, and it was an album he had mainly recorded in 1979 in Switzerland. *Rock 'n ' Roll Prophet* was released at the back end of 1982 on Rick's own Moon Records label. It combined the vocal material that he had released in 1980 on A & M with other instrumental pieces that aren't too different in style to his 1979 *Rhapsodies* album, particularly in terms of that albums lighthearted tone. There is one more vocal track with Rick singing, the wry 'Maybe '80' – although one suspects its humorous tone hides a rather more personal message. The instrumental tracks are much better than their reputation suggest, containing a lot of analogue instruments and some excellent Minimoog – especially on 'Stalemate' (although that track wasn't featured on the original vinyl version). The enhanced version (with a 'plus' added) released many years later, which contains several tracks recorded at the time but not on the album, generally suffers a tad from over-egging the same pudding. Less is definitely more, in this case. The track 'Early Warning' contains material that was repurposed for 'Golden Age', one of the tracks that was unfinished during the Yes Paris sessions. One final note. This album has a cover, with photography by Nina Carter. To say that it's in dubious taste would be putting it mildly.

Rick has always been good value on TV. As a guest on chat shows, his many anecdotes always stand him in good stead, with the added bonus that he will be happy to tinkle the ivories on cue. Many will remember his many media appearances when David Bowie died in 2016 when Rick's genuine warmth – and skill at the piano – lead to a late flowering of his own solo career.

However, there have also been a few attempts to launch a presenting career. One such was the Channel 4 show *Gastank*, which aired at the back end of 1982 and at the start of 1983. Rick co-presented with fellow keysman Tony Ashton. This was an interesting pairing since Ashton came from a much more blues-orientated background. The two conducted interviews with their celebrity guests, which included old bluesmen like Eric Burdon and Alvin Lee, Godley and Crème, Rick Parfitt of Status Quo, John Enwhistle of The Who, Phil Lynott, Steve Harley, Roy Wood and Steve Hackett. The format was a mixture of live performances, with the musicians including a house band that included Chaz Cronk and Tony Fernandez – and those interviews.

The whole series is now available to watch on YouTube and an album of the music was released in 2016. Musically, there's much to enjoy, despite the slightly low-fi nature of the audio transfer – some of the performances are unique, and the standard of musicianship is high. While the music has often been described as 'impromptu', it's clear that there must at least have been some rehearsal. The problems lie in two areas. Firstly, neither Wakeman or Ashton are natural presenters, and when improvising, they sound like they are chatting in a pub (although that was clearly the point, thus the name *Gastank,* which in this context means a sleazy place to talk or 'gas', although the Urban Dictionary has a number of less savoury definitions. I dare you to look them up) and when reading pre-prepared material, they both sound amateurish. The tone of the shows is overwhelmingly 'matey' – these are musicians using their little black books to get their mates along for a pint and a natter in a TV studio, and it feels like it.

Secondly – and this is not a criticism of the show itself at all – how on earth did this ever get commissioned? In 1982, these were the least fashionable musicians on the planet. Had the shows been broadcast five years earlier, they might have been greeted with some excitement, but in 1982? It stood no chance. A series of six episodes was always going to be the extent of its run.

Nonetheless, despite being a show out of time, I'd recommend to anyone that they dig into this curiosity. It may be a relic, but it's a fascinating one.

1983 – It's All About the Numbers

Fast forward several months with Cinema now nearing completion of the first cut of their album, and Jon Dee was played seven finished tracks by Trevor Horn. Jon was invited to dinner with Horn by the latter's engineer Gary Langan, who had already been involved in *Drama*. The songs that Jon heard that night included 'It's Over', which was dropped and appeared as a bonus track of the Rhino reissue of *90125* – a somewhat schmaltzy Rabin power ballad. He also heard an Anderson-free version of 'Hold On', with more prominent bass and Trevor Horn's backing vocals placed a lot more prominently. He also heard 'Changes', 'Hearts' and 'It Can Happen'. He also mentions that he heard a very long track, presumably the legendary piece 'Time', which included the short instrumental 'Cinema' that was recorded live at Air Studios (rather than Sarm West, as most of the album was). This piece has gone down in Yes-lore as 'the track that never was', but it seems likely that not only did it exist in people's heads, but there may also be a recorded version out there that has yet to see the light of day. Indeed, when the band first hit the studio, the first two tracks attempted were 'Time' and the far less mythical 'Changes', according to subsequent discussions between Jon Dee and Alan White, plus 'Hearts' built up from Tony Kaye's initial synth riff.

However, Trevor Rabin reports that Tony Kaye and Trevor Horn didn't always see eye to eye, and Kaye did not see out the album sessions. He told *Rock Candy*:

> ...he [Trevor Horn] told me that Tony had gone back home. He said that he and Chris Squire had discussed Tony's position, and they also talked to Phil Carson about it. They'd all agreed that Tony wasn't working out and it was best to let him go. I was furious. I was just as much a part of the band as anyone else and I told Trevor that at the very least, I should have been consulted before the decision was taken.

This meant that Rabin was now expected to play the majority of the keyboard parts on the album, although there's still some of Tony in there, particularly on 'Cinema' and his 'baby', 'Hearts'.

90125
Personnel:
Jon Anderson: vocals

Chris Squire; bass guitars, vocals
Trevor Rabin: guitars, keyboards, vocals
Alan White: drums, percussion, backing vocals, Fairlight CMI
Tony Kaye: keyboards
Trevor Horn: production
Yes: production on Hold On
Gary Langan: engineering
Jonathan Jeczalik: keyboard programming
Dave Lawson: keyboard programming
Bob Ludwig: mastering
Garry Mouat: album sleeve
Released: 7 November 1983
Recorded: November 1982 – July 1983
Studio   SARM and AIR Studios, London
Highest chart places: UK: 16, USA
Tracklist: 1.Owner of a Lonely Heart (Rabin/Anderson/Squire/Horn) 2. Hold On
(Rabin/ Anderson/Squire) 3. It Can Happen (Squire/Anderson/Rabin) 4. Changes
(Rabin/Anderson/ White) 5. Cinema (Squire/Rabin/White/Tony Kaye) 6. Leave It
(Squire/Rabin/Horn) 7. Our Song (Anderson/Squire/Rabin/White   ) 8. City of Love
(Rabin/Anderson) 9. Hearts (Anderson/Squire/Rabin/White/Kaye)

Having heard at least part of it, Jon Dee is certain that there is a version
of *90125* that exists without Jon Anderson at all. This was sent to the
record company in the spring of 1983, and it was this 'version' that led
to speculation that the band needed a singer and that Jon Anderson
might be the man for the job. One strongly suspects that it was not just
Anderson's past history with Yes and Squire that led to this decision. Had
Anderson faded into obscurity after his departure from the band in 1980,
then he might not have been considered. However, he had not and at the
end of 1982, his profile had increased once again with the hugely popular
'I'll Find My Way Home' single with Vangelis.

Rabin suggested to *Rock Candy* that the idea to bring Jon back came
from Squire, but it's more likely it was a mutual decision concocted
between 'the suits' (mainly Phil Carson) and Squire, based on a need for a
more commercial product – and to call the band Yes. The latter move was
– understandably – objected to by Rabin, but more commercially-minded
opinions, including Squire and the rest of the band, held sway.

The first thing to do was to get hold of Anderson and to play him the
material. Squire drove to Anderson's rented house in London – the

nomadic singer was in town because he had been recording his third album with Vangelis (about which more shortly), but Anderson's wife Jennifer wouldn't let Squire in due to an old grudge between the two men's wives, so Anderson listened to the songs in Squire's car. He liked what he heard and agreed to be part of the band. It was there and then – claims Anderson – that the first idea of calling the band Yes came up, although this is disputed. Rabin claims the decision was made later. Anderson says he was joining Yes from the word go. This seems likely, particularly as we've already speculated that this was always Phil Carson's plan anyway.

How, then, does a man come into the making of an album to sing lead vocals and end up with seven writing credits? Rabin told *Rock Candy:*

Jon earned every one of those credits. He did change some things around in the songs, but he was always very sensitive in how he did it. Jon adjusted the lyrics in certain numbers so they'd fit better with his singing style – and the alterations he made improved what we had.

It's very clear that while he had very little time to make his mark, the inspired fairy dust that Anderson sprinkled over the album made a decent effort considerably better. The best record we have of this is in the two released version of 'It Can Happen'. The 'Cinema version', which has Squire singing lead, had a different – and rather more plodding – verse than the finished mix, Anderson's replacement providing some useful and rather more sophisticated tension before the 'release' of the pre-chorus and chorus. The original is a rather more leisurely take on the song anyway, missing some of the technical bells and whistles of the finished version, so one suspects that this might not have represented the final pre-Anderson mix anyway, but it's still a stark contrast. In the main, though, as Horn points out, 'He couldn't unwrite the songs, although he did his best.'

Elsewhere, it's Anderson's distinctiveness as a lead – and backing – vocalist that really makes a difference, not to mention the natural chemistry he always had with Squire's talents as a harmony vocalist, best heard on 'Hold On' (listen out for Horn – he's still in there somewhere on the choruses). It's the contract between those two vocalists that works the best, while Rabin's backing vocals are used sparingly when he's not singing lead; going back to 'Hold On' he's more prominent in the latter part of the song as an added vocal texture when the track builds in intensity.

This page: Despite some 'disinformation' over the years regarding his status in the band, in this article from *Sounds* in November 1983, it's very clear: Eddie Jobson is the keyboard player for Yes. *(David Watkinson Collection)*

It wasn't possible for Anderson to cover all Rabin's vocal parts, and he's largely absent from the intricate vocal arrangement for the quirky US hit 'Leave It', except towards the end of the song, where his upper-register voice is cleverly used to add intensity, while Rabin handles most of the lead vocals, with the odd line slipped in by Anderson. The contrast also works well on the proggy classic 'Changes', with its opening percussion part written by White. The song had been arranged within an inch of its life well before Anderson's arrival – one suspects that the Cinema version of this was already pretty sensational. Anderson's role is more straightforward here – lead on the chorus with backup from Squire, and add the odd lead vocal as a contrast to Rabin's. Meanwhile, Rabin gave up his lead vocals entirely on the heavy 'City of Love' and the underrated 'Our Song' to the diminutive vocalist.

While 'Hearts' is not my favourite of Yes songs, I do get that it was seen as a nod towards 'classic Yes'. Alongside 'Owner' it is one of two songs that Anderson has adopted as his own for later performances and was played live by the band as late as the year 2000. He's more integrated into the vocal arrangement alongside Squire and Rabin. Whether by happy accident, plan or a bit of both, it's the contrast of all these voices – plus White's and an uncredited Horn – that really lifts the album from the good to the great.

As for the rest of the band, while it's Rabin's AOR-orientated, overdriven guitar lines that dominate, the contrast with his clean playing – in 'Changes', for instance – cannot be understated. His keyboard playing is functional and if anything has dated the album, it's the choice of sounds in that department. Squire and White demonstrate that dumbing down a touch doesn't mean that they are repressed completely. There are still plenty of Yes-isms to enjoy. And then there's 'that single...'

'Owner of a Lonely Heart', which opens the album with a mind-altering bang, whether you enjoyed the music of previous incarnations of Yes or not, was almost an afterthought. It was brought into the sessions quite late on when the Trevors Horn and Rabin were listening to demos at Rabin's apartment. The guitarist had gone to the bathroom, leaving the producer to listen to the demos on his own. As soon as he heard the song – which is the version that can be heard on Rabin's *90124* album – he smelled a hit. The song is essentially 'there' in acoustic form, although the final version required a lot of manipulation, with Horn and Squire rewriting the verses and, on arrival, Anderson adding some lyrical touches. Listen carefully and you can hear Anderson's 'eagle in the sky' being shot down – a moment of wry protest from Horn at some of Jon's changes.

The song is full of production tricks, twists and turns. Horn left no stone unturned to almost 'force' the song to be a hit. White's snare was sampled, tuned to a top A, as Horn was a fan of Stuart Copeland's drum sound (the Police were hugely popular), rather than the 'big' drum sound that Rabin was after, for which Mutt Lange, Rabin's South African friend and mentor, was largely responsible. 'Sounds like a fucking pea on a barrel', said White's drum tech Nu Nu Whiting at the time.

The horn stabs were the height of sophistication in 1983 – again, sampling technology flexing its muscles. The samples used came from the James Brown horns, recorded for the Malcolm McClaren album that Trevor Horn had been working on prior to working with Yes. Horn is full of praise for the creativity of Alan White, who plays the distinctive ascending pattern on the Fairlight. Another imaginitive touch was Rabin's guitar solo which sees it doubled in fifths via a harmonizer pedal. There's even a crowd-pleasing key change just before the fade-out. To give the lead vocal to Anderson must have seemed an obvious choice, but it's the contrast between his strident vocal and Rabin's treated counterpoint ('much better than a...') that really impresses. To get such a disciplined performance from a rock band shows what an impressive man-manager Horn is. Forcing the 'rock-isms' out of Rabin and Squire must have been a challenge. Kaye had gone home to LA by the time it was recorded.

Finally, there was an album that everyone could be proud of. How does it stand up? Whether you enjoy the album depends largely on how you feel about this style of music generally. To me, it's a terrific record that does what it set out to do perfectly – there's absolutely no filler, and the fairy dust that Anderson provides (despite the odd cheesy moment) both in the writing and vocal departments makes a massive difference. Would the album have been as successful without him? Almost certainly not.

The Keyboard Player That Never Was

However, there was one more twist in the tale. Readers may have noticed that the name 'Phil Carson' has replaced 'Brian Lane' in this story, and by this point Carson had put a huge amount of time and personal investment into the development of this 'new' band. Lane was no longer part of the set up, having gone onto to concentrate on Asia. With Kaye having left, a keyboard player was needed so that the band could tour. Eddie Jobson was by this point already very experienced, having been a member of UK (with John Wetton and Bill Bruford) and Jethro Tull, and lived in the USA. Jobson claims already to have been offered the keyboard player's job with Cinema in early 1983 (presumably when Kaye first departed) and turned it down, running foul of the difficulties he'd already had as part of the EG management set-up.

However, liking the new album when Rabin played it to him later in the year, he agreed to join as a full member and attended the mastering of the album with Rabin. He now takes up the story via a piece from 2007 that appears on *Yesfans.com*. Jobson calls his account an 'abridged' one, and I have further abridged it, taking out some of his more insulting comments (particularly regarding Chris Squire) that, while they may have the ring of truth about them, also feel exaggerated. It is clear, however, that the band were already worrying about their credibility as Yes.

We got together in a rehearsal room and thrashed through a few tunes, including 'Roundabout' (actually not knowing the song too well, I had to figure out Rick's tricky keyboard parts on the spot – no easy task). But everyone seemed happy, so I returned to the U.S. as a full member of Yes and with a world tour only two or three months away. There was virtually no contact with anyone for several weeks as I learned all the Yes material in my home studio.

The illusion of equal membership soon became apparently false, especially once the filming of the 'Owner of a Lonely Heart' video took place. Despite my considerable experiences with Roxy, Zappa, UK, and Tull (a wonderful group of guys who treated me with considerable respect), and with more than 30 albums and a self-managed solo career under my belt, no one was interested in any wisdom I may have been able to impart, on any subject, even on the keyboard rig design which had already been decided upon. But I had made a commitment and I wanted to see it through.

Several weeks later, back in the U.S. where I continued to work on the considerable Yes repertoire, I did finally receive a phone call from someone – it was the manager who had been given the unceremonious task of informing me that Tony Kaye was re-joining the group and would be sharing keyboard duties with me. No discussion, no conferring; a done deal. And the reason? They needed three original members to put to rest a dispute with Brian Lane (their old manager), Steve Howe and Rick Wakeman regarding the legitimacy of the new band using the 'Yes' name. [There were] no apologies, just take it or leave it, so I hearkened to the words of their own song and chose to 'leave it'.

Looking back at the UK promotion for *90125*, which appeared to coincide with the release of the album at the end of November 1983, it's very clear that Jobson is the keyboard player. He appears in all the promotional photographs, and his rehearsals with the band 'a couple of months ago', so presumably sometime in the late Summer, are referred to in glowing terms in an article in *Sounds* by Philip Bell. Anderson reported:

> ... Eddie and Trevor were doing things without thinking. It was marvellous to watch. Ten years ago, it was very difficult to get hold of two musicians that would do battle on that sort of level.

So, it seems the hierarchy in the band and those almost inevitable managerial and legal issues put paid to the participation of a hugely talented player who might have offered up something different to the band.

Rabin's version of events differs somewhat from Jobson's, suggesting in *Rock Candy* that in the end, Jobson was never a formal member of the band, and that they decided to go with a different style keyboard player for musical reasons. He claims that the only reason that Jobson appears in the video for 'Owner' is because he had rehearsed with the band the day before. There is no mention of legal issues around the usage of the name Yes and also no mention of a possible two keyboard player set up. It's certainly a bold reinterpretation of the known facts since we have the evidence that Jobson was featured in the pre-release press coverage. It is likely, however, that it was Rabin as much as anyone who invited Kaye to rejoin since Squire felt that their relationship had been tainted by what had happened during recording, the implication being that Squire had sided with Horn when the latter expressed dissatisfaction in Kaye's playing. Just days after the album had been released, it seemed, Kaye was back in the band.

It's a Hit!

The album was released in November 1983 to good reviews and almost instant commercial success. Rather than the traditional Roger Dean cover (since Dean was 'with' Asia) the band went with a futuristic, computer generated design by Garry Mouat, variations on which were also used for the 12" single releases of 'Owner', 'Leave It' and 'It Can Happen'. These releases followed the 1980s fashion for esoteric, impressionistic dance mixes, which the listener probably wouldn't play too often.

The huge success of the album, particularly in the US, where the album peaked at number five, was spurred by the huge success of 'Owner Of A Lonely Heart'. As often happened during that period, the track was a relatively slow burner in the USA, doing well in the *Billboard* Rock Chart, but gradually climbing the pop chart, seemingly becalmed at number four at the end of December, then rising to two and then one for two weeks in January 1984.

A similar pattern followed in most territories, with the song reaching the top ten in Canada and all over Europe. Only in the UK did it not do so well, rising to 28 in December then fading away swiftly, the album only achieving the number 16 position. The reason? Very simply, Yes were the least fashionable band in the UK in a time of genuine pop creativity. All the promotional bucks in the world were not going to get the band a number one in their home territory.

Of considerable assistance with the band's success were the three videos the band recorded for their singles. The band had already recorded promos in the past, of course, but without much quality. 'Wonderous Stories' had been a UK hit, and there had also been promos for 'Don't Kill The Whale' and 'Madrigal' from *Tormato*, plus mimed live performance promos for two songs from *Drama*. This was a different era, of course, and the most seen was the Storm Thorgerson-directed video for 'Owner', starring actor Danny Webb. The video was quickly re-edited to exclude Jobson as far as possible – Jobson appears in the initial performance section and then in the London rooftop scene at the end of the video. Presumably, he also had his own 'animal transformation' scene, but this would have been easier to edit out. It's a bold video – but what does it mean? Not much, one suspects.

A second video was shot for the song after Tony Kaye had rejoined, recorded in some sort of studio-set tropical scene. It's terrible. As some wag remarked on YouTube: 'They blew the whole budget in four parrots.' Enough said.

The video for 'Leave It', again with Kaye back in the band, made use of the advances in video technology in a way that has dated badly, but nonetheless is a least distinctive, while 'It Can Happen' – which features a lot of Chris Squire – again returns to safe ground with a mixture of band performance and video effects. They are very much 'of their time'.

Steve Howe was astonished by this new take on Yes, remarking on the *Yes Classic Artists* DVD about how he felt on first hearing *90125*:

I was listening to 'Owner of a Lonely Heart' and thinking, 'Yes has really changed. Change the guitarist; change the whole group.' I never realised that would happen. I thought they were going to be the same group with a different guitarist. I didn't conceive it as being anything like Yes, it was more like Asia in a way. This was a new thing for me to get used to, that while in Asia, Yes existed as well.

Asia – *Alpha*

Personnel:
John Wetton: bass, vocals
Steve Howe: guitars
Geoff Downes: keyboards
Carl Palmer: drums
Released: 8 August 1983
Recorded: Le Studio (Montreal, Canada) and Manta Sound (Toronto, Canada) February-May 1983
Produced by: Mike Stone
Engineers: Mike Stone, Paul Northfield
Cover Illustration: Roger Dean
All tracks written by Wetton / Downes except (2) by Wetton
Highest chart position: UK: 5, US: 6
Tracklisting 1. Don't Cry 2. The Smile Has Left Your Eyes 3. Never in a Million Years 4. My Own Time (I'll Do What I Want) 5. The Heat Goes On 6. Eye to Eye 7. The Last to Know 8. True Colors 9. Midnight Sun 10. Open Your Eyes

Asia, of course, were a year ahead of the new Yes. They had a hugely successful album, hit singles, Grammy nominations and a well-received tour behind them. The cash was rolling in for everyone. And what do you do when you're a British musician and there's cash coming in? You take a year away from Britain for tax purposes, obviously!

The band went to the frozen wastes of Quebec in the winter of 1983 to record the next album. While Howe, Downes and Palmer flew in and out at various times to record their parts, Wetton stayed in Canada with producer Mike Stone. A bitingly cold Canadian winter proved not to be the most inspirational environment for the under-pressure Wetton. Furthermore, both management and label put the band under pressure to produce more hits, seeing the Downes / Wetton partnership as being the way to do it. This, of course, froze out Howe, who quite rightly saw himself as being a vital part of the writing team that had created a hugely successful debut. Indeed, part of the success of the first album was the way that the material and arrangements – some of which has been originated several years ago by Wetton – were developed and refined organically. With the band rarely in the same room at the same time for album two and the Downes / Wetton partnership urged to produce all the material, this organic approach disappeared almost completely. After a short stint completing his vocals in Toronto, the album was (Wetton thought) complete. He commented to his biographer Kim Dancha:

> I remember being absolutely exhausted and pretty much at the end of my tether when the songs were completed for that record. All the recording had been done and it was just such a relief to get over it.

But Wetton's trial wasn't quite over, with John Kalodner, on hearing the album, telling Wetton that he felt the singer 'had another song in him.' That song was to be the lead single 'Don't Cry'. As well as having his material largely ignored, Howe was aware at the time that the album wasn't really to his taste, describing it in his autobiography as, 'quite commercial – not terribly prog, with many repeated choruses and few instrumental sections.'

Steve is right about that, but it was not so much the material that disappointed me when I first heard the album in 1983. First of all, when I opened up the package, with its pleasing Roger Dean cover, it was pressed on the flimsiest bit of vinyl I had ever experienced. Not far away from a flexidisk. Secondly – and more importantly – it sounded *awful*, trebly and almost distorted. Momentarily, I assumed that the record I had bought was faulty – what a disappointment.

Listening to it again, I understand why I felt like that. I still feel it now. The problem with the album overall is not just in the arrangements, but in the way *Alpha* seems to have been mixed to sound good on AM radio, not on a decent stereo. It feels like the label – for it must have been them – didn't care about the listener as long as as many songs as possible sounded good on the radio. Guitars and keyboards get lost in a wall of sound while Wetton struggles to be heard through all the reverb on his voice and as for Palmer, it could almost be anyone behind the kit. Regardless of the quality of the material here – and there's no doubt that there's some decent songwriting on offer – what's the point to writing a good song if the mix makes your ears bleed? How is that a good thing? While I realise that not everybody feels the same way as I do, to me, it was an utter disaster, and it put me off the band – pretty much for life.

So, what of this turkey on a track-by-track basis? From a material point of view, it's pretty decent on first examination. 'Don't Cry' is a good, commercial pop song, deserving of its US chart success, but no more than that. 'The Smile Has Left Your Eyes' – a real winner on the 1982 tour – is reduced to a short power ballad, which goes up to eleven within seconds of its promising opening. The album then descends into mediocrity, with several songs that achieve a certain level of tunefulness without setting the world alight. 'Never In a Million Years' has some good moments for Howe, while 'I'll Do What I Want' at least stretches out a little and the side one closer, 'The Heat Goes On,' is the only song up to that point that allows a genuinely expanded arrangement in the style of the first album.

Side two opens tunefully with 'Eye to Eye', although it's been hideously edited for the album just as Downes and Howe are getting busy, while 'The Last To Know' also has some merit, with a bold, proggy middle section. 'True Colours' continues the pattern – a nice song desperately in need of a proggier arrangement. If the album has a potential classic, it's the terrific 'Midnight Sun', although the power of this beautiful song is neutered by the insipid sonics, with way too much reverb on Wetton's voice. On 'Open Your Eyes', the band are finally allowed to stretch out, but it's the imaginative arrangement that's the real winner, and the listener desperately wants it to sound as good as the debut – but it doesn't.

Two tracks were left off the album and appeared as B-sides and on later compilations. 'Daylight' opened the set on the 1983 tour, and it's a splendid up-tempo piece, while 'Lying To Yourself' was the only Howe / Wetton co-write recorded. In truth, it's fine but nothing more than that, with a melody typical of Howe's writing. It would have made a good album track by way of variation from some of the more mediocre and homogenous songs on the album itself, but it's hardly a lost classic.

This time out, the band's tour took in just North America. However, aside from worsening relations within the group, with the four travelling to shows separately, there were other problems. First of all, while the success of the debut had brought in a mixture of fans from the musician's other bands and new supporters, attracted by the hits, many of these new fans were mayflies, who moved on to the next big thing after a while.

Furthermore, the band fell between two stools. They were too big for theatres, but not yet with the following, which in those days would be generated over several years of touring as Yes had done, to sell out arenas outside the East and West coasts. They were playing in venues they simply could not fill.

Howe reports that musical differences were also starting to show and that live arrangements were starting to become confused. The band was falling apart before their very eyes, and Wetton was blamed – rightly or wrongly. The band postponed the rest of the tour. Opinions really differ as to what precisely went on at this point and given that this is a book about Yes and its members, we won't delve into the whys and wherefores. But – for now, at least – Wetton was out.

However, there was a further problem. The band were committed to two shows at the Nippon Budokan in Japan in early December to be shown on MTV. Indeed, filming of the pre-show segments, which included interviews with all of the band, had been started while Wetton was still present. What could they do? Palmer invited his former ELP colleague Greg Lake to take over the vocalist/bassist slot for the shows, and just as well – he was possibly the only musician with the talent and stature to fill the role if truth be told.

The live performance is available to watch on YouTube, and it's well worth catching for a few reasons. Firstly, Lake is astonishingly good, giving the material plenty of his own character – he was, arguably, a better vocalist than Wetton. Secondly, Downes' keyboard set up is mind-blowing, arranged in a long line of stacked instruments (rather than as three parts of a square, as he has it now). It's a bold rig that must have been challenging to play. As the year ended, the band – while grateful for Lake's help getting them out of a tight spot – decided not to continue the arrangement.

Rick Wakeman – G'olé

Personnel:
Rick Wakeman: keyboards, writing, arrangements, production
Jackie McAuley: acoustic guitars
Mitch Dalton: acoustic guitars
Tony Fernandez: drums
Recorded and mixed at Berwick Street Studios, London, Olympic Studios, Barnes, Jacobs Studio, Farnham
Released: March 1983

Tracklisting: 1. International Flag 2. The Dove (opening ceremony) 3. Wayward Spirit 4. Latin Reel (Theme From G'olé) 5. Red Island 6. Spanish Holiday 7. No Possible 8. Shadows 9. Black Pearls 10. Frustration 11. Spanish Montage 12. G'olé

Rick Wakeman – *Cost of Living*

Personnel:
Rick Wakeman: keyboards, music, production
Hereward Kaye: vocals
Jackie McAuley: guitar
John Gustafson: bass
Robert Powell: narration
Tony Fernandez: drums, percussion
Tim Rice: lyrics
Released: 1983
Tracklisting: 1. Twij 2. Pandamonia 3. Gone But Not Forgotten 4. One For The Road 5. Bedtime Stories 6. Happening Man 7. Shakespeare Run 8. Monkey Nuts 9. Elegy - Written in a Country Churchyard

1983 was a more productive year for Rick, with a couple of projects coming to fruition while he bedded into his modest life of domesticity with Nina Carter and the difficult birth of their first child (Rick's fourth), Jemma. The first was *G'olé,* his soundtrack for the film of the 1982 Football World Cup. In the modern era TV coverage can be found around the clock and such official films, when they are produced at all, no longer have the traction they once did. *G'ole* received a modest theatre release in the spring of 1983. The tournament had been played in Spain, and was won by Italy, who beat West Germany 3-1 in the final. The album was released as part of his contract with Charisma, so was well distributed. I bought it on vinyl at the time.

Given that the music was written and performed to accompany cues in the movie, the various short-ish tracks stand up pretty well on their own. There is – as one might expect – a strong Spanish theme to the compositions, and while none of the themes are anywhere near as memorable as, say, *White Rock,* meaning that even die-hard Wakeman fans are unlikely to drag this one out very often, it still stands up well. Tony Fernandez provides drums, as usual.

Given the relative success of *1984,* for Rick's next (and, as it turned out, final) album for Charisma, *Cost of Living,* he was reunited with Tim Rice, who provided the lyrics. The album is a mixture of songs – without a concept this time – and instrumentals, including one classic that had really stood the test of time, the lovely 'Gone but Not Forgotten'. Singer for this one album was former Café Society vocalist (and later a Flying Picket) Hareward Kaye. Typical of Rick at the time, he met Kaye in a pub. An unusual vocalist, Kaye's Roger Water's-style delivery certainly gives the vocal tracks an edge, even if the songwriting itself isn't Rick's best, albeit very much in a rocked-up style.

As Rick himself pointed out on his website:

It has too much variation within the music for me to be really happy about it, and again I ended up in a studio that I really didn't like that was picked by the record company at the time and so I couldn't change. There's a mixture of great playing and some very poor playing as well. Most disappointing is the piano sound, as the piano in the studio was cheap and nasty.

Certainly, there's a real contrast between the gentle, romantic instrumentals and the hard-rocking, prog-punk of the songs. But most out of place is the instrumental setting of Thomas Grey's 'Elegy: Written in a Country Churchyard' with narration by actor Robert Powell. This is an odd experience since during the softer moments, the combination of spoken word and music works well, but as soon as the band kicks in, the poetry is rendered indistinct at best, so all the listener gets is an impression. It's a strange listening experience on an otherwise decent and somewhat underrated album.

To tie in with the album, Rick recorded a TV special that included tracks from the album. This doesn't seem to have survived in its entity, but the 'Bedtime Stories' section – with off-key toddlers – being all that's available on YouTube. It's heavily stylized stuff. The track has been re-recorded and Rick sits in tails at the piano in a typical BBCTV light entertainment studio set, probably miming, while three moppets sit on a bed. It's a diabetes diagnosis in three and a half minutes.

Sadly, this was to be Rick's last major-label offering for forty years...

Jon and Vangelis – *Private Collection*

Personnel:
Jon Anderson: Vocals
Vangelis: Keyboards, Synthesisers, Programming
Dick Morrissey: Saxophone on 'And When the Night Comes'

Music composed by Vangelis
Lyrics written by Jon Anderson
Arranged and produced by Vangelis
Highest chart places: UK: 22. USA: 148
Tracklisting: 1. Italian Song 2. And When the Night Comes 3. Deborah 4. Polonaise
5. He Is Sailing 6. Horizon

If both Jon and Vangelis' first two albums had had elements of the contrived about them, given the speed with which they had both been recorded and the improvisatory nature of their construction, then the duo's third album was to be a slightly different affair.

Things were different now. Vangelis, via his celebrated soundtrack album to the Oscar-winning movie *Chariots Of Fire* was now a famous man – even if he hated the idea. As a duo, they had two hit albums and two top ten singles behind them. There had been a power shift in their favour.

The album was recorded in London and Paris in the early part of 1983 – it was during the London sessions that Chris Squire made contact with Jon with a view to becoming involved in the Cinema project – and *Private Collection* was released in July. It's a much more polished and considered album than the first two, with Vangelis clearly putting more time and effort into his compositions and post-production. It's nicely structured, too, with the first side of vinyl dedicated to shorter tracks and the second side one long piece in 'Horizon'. The overall tone is sophisticated and restrained. Indeed, the whole album is extremely symphonic, with string synths to the fore. But there's very little of the joyous exuberance or indeed humour of the first two albums. And they are missed.

In fact, if you were an A & R man looking at the album from a commercial point of view, you might say, 'I don't hear a single'. And you'd be right. This is born out by the sheer number of songs from the album that were released across various territories, to modest success at best. 'He Is Sailing' was the choice in the UK, reaching a disappointing 61, while 'Deborah' was released in Spain, 'Polonaise' in France and 'When the Night Comes' released almost everywhere except Britain. The regular B-side was the non-album 'Song Is'.

From a lyrical point of view, Anderson covers fairly well-trodden ground, focusing on the divine ('He Is Sailing', 'Polonaise' and 'Horizon') and family affection with 'Deborah', which is essentially his reaction to getting a letter from his eldest daughter.

'Italian Song', the charming opener, is essentially Anderson's version of an Italian operatic aria, accompanied by gentle keyboards, while the plodding 'And When the Night Comes' could do with a more boisterous tempo, despite some nice sax from Dick Morrissey. Heaven knows why the record company thought this was suitable material for a single release. 'Deborah' is tuneful, but another very restrained piece and as for 'Polonaise' – yes, it's another ballad. Vangelis adds some welcome piano and percussion, but by this point, the listener is begging for something with a bit of life. Thankfully this does come with wonderful 'He Is Sailing', which is the first track to reach any sort of reasonable tempo. The obvious single, if there is one, it's possible that some territories were put off by the song's overtly Christian subject matter, but it's wonderful anyway – perhaps the only 'classic' on the album.

'Horizon' opens intriguingly, like the soundtrack to a lost spy movie, and Anderson's opening vocal also works nicely – this, so far, is enticing stuff, and when the main hook arrives, it hits home. This might have worked nicely as a six or seven-minute track, but it repeats until the nine and a half minute mark, at which point Vangelis intervenes in symphonic, romantic style for a mid-section which sees the pace drop and Anderson singing in far more reflective style, although Vangelis' piano playing is excellent. A burst of sound five minutes from the end promises a change of pace, but no, this leads to – well, more reflection and synths that tinkle to a quiet end to what, it has to be said, is an almost somnambulistically quiet album.

Opinions differ about this record, so don't take my lukewarm opinion as gospel. Gary Hill of *Allmusic.com* said:

Truly the nearly 23-minute 'Horizon' really feels a lot like a modern symphony. It is definitely the culmination of their work together, their most ambitious effort. The shorter cuts on the album all have their moments and surely hold up to anything from the previous releases, but 'Horizon' stands far above them all. It combines the best elements of Anderson's work in Yes with the electronically classically tinged stylings of Vangelis to produce a work that is near-masterpiece in its quality. It is a life-affirming, positive piece.

But Prog Leviathan on *Progarchives.com* dismisses the album as being for fans only:

Long, airy, forgettable, and so '80s new-age as to sound painfully dated, this one is absolutely for fans of either of these musicians only, who will probably find a lot to like in the slow, delicate, textures of Vangelis' keyboard and Anderson's (sadly) unremarkable and sombre vocals.

David Watkinson had the pleasure of visiting Vangelis in his London studio just after the recording of *Private Collection*:

Part of my 'world' as a fan in the 1980s was in helping out with various UK Yes fanzines. The fanzine world was just starting due to the increasing indifference, or is some cased hatred, of prog rock in the music press. I provided photos, crosswords, comments and maybe the odd interview and bit of artwork to a healthy, flourishing world of fanzines such as *YesMusic, Tizz Music, Relayer* and *Sound Chaser*, all run by Yes heads – a dedicated bunch indeed.

On one occasion, I found myself in central London behind Marble Arch to visit Vangelis's Nemo Recording Studios. I went there with Jon Anderson's personal assistant, John Martin to write an article. Like many places in a city, the entrance was industrial and nondescript, but what a different world was hidden inside. Walking into Vangelis's studio felt like a cross between visiting an art gallery combined with a keyboard and musical instrument store. Everywhere you looked was a feast for the eye. There were gold discs, paintings, speakers, keyboards... and more keyboards. I felt I was in the presence of someone very special.

John and I spoke and then he introduced me to Vangelis, a gentle giant and a living legend. Pleasantries over, I was allowed to walk around the studio gazing at the astonishing equipment. I count myself a very lucky man to have experienced it.

1984 – A Tour to End All Tours

If you had the opportunity to experience arena gigs in the 1980s – and your author had that privilege a great deal in that decade – you will remember it as a time when 'the show' was everything. Huge piles of cash were poured into stage designs and lighting shows, while all signs of 'rock and roll' trappings were often dispensed with where these were not an essential aspect of a band's image. A band's backline was sometimes hidden so that if a musician needed to make an adjustment mid-set, they would need to walk off stage to do it. More likely, there was a minion to do that for them. Musicians that were not part of the 'official band' were also to be found offstage and unseen by the paying public. Often these were keyboard players, but sometimes backup guitarists, percussionists and even vocalists could be found plying their trade behind a backdrop or perhaps below the stage.

So it was with our heroes. A huge tour was planned with an expensive show made for big venues. In the USA, this was the band's staple gig; the massive tours of 1978 and 1979 had seeing them play 'in the round', and the 1980 tour had also seen them playing these sorts of venues, albeit to smaller crowds. Now the band were 'pop stars' and touring in a different, more colourful era. This was going to be huge.

Even in the 1970s, Yes had used the occasional sound enhancement via Eddie Offord at the live sound desk. However, the issues with the *90125* tour were complicated. As well as a sophisticated stage set, the audiences of 1984 didn't expect any aural rough edges either, and with *90125* containing some complex and well-crafted keyboard and vocal arrangements that would need to be reproduced on stage. With Kaye not the most spectacular technician and with his hands full playing many of the lead parts required of him during the set, the decision was made to bring in a second musician who would enhance the live sound from below the stage. Casey Young was an in-demand session synthesizer player, having already worked with Gary Wright, Michael Sembello and Madonna, plus playing on the soundtrack for the movie *Staying Alive.* By 1984, he was building a strong reputation, not specifically for his chops, but because the rig he had designed for himself gave him access to textures and sounds that other contemporary keyboard players could not match. We would go on to a future career as both player and programmer, most famously on Michael Jackson's *Bad* album in 1987. He explained what his initial role was to be for the *90125* tour, and how it expanded on the *Yes Music Podcast* in 2020:

I got a call in 1983 from Tim Myer, a guitar tec deluxe for many bands, and he knew my keyboard design chops and my synthesizer programming. He ask me to design a system for Tony Kaye, and to reproduce the sounds on that record [*90125*]. So, they hired me to put that rig together, which was a really fancy rig for 1983. If you remember, midi [a digital system that allows instruments to talk to each other, still very much in use today] was just coming in, but it wasn't implemented on everything, so we had our work cut out. They asked me to programme it, and then I went back for rehearsals to get Tony going on it. About halfway through rehearsals at Clair Brothers [the company providing Yes' sound system for the tour], they wanted Tony to add another sound to the song 'Hearts', and Tony said 'I'm full up, all my presets are loaded, I can't do it.' Chris looked at me and said, 'He can'. I said, 'I can't go – I've got sessions to do!' So, we talked about it, and finally, Jon said to me, 'Run away with the circus; give it a try for a couple of days, see if you like it.' Two years later, I was still playing with the band.

Given that Eddie Jobson reported that his planned rig had already been designed for him, it seems that this must have been part of Casey's design as well. Casey went on to explain in a bit more detail what his role on the tour was:

You have to bear in mind that I was an afterthought. If this had happened a few months later, I would probably have been on stage. For the next tour I was due to do, which would have been for *Big Generator,* I was due to be on stage. Chris had it all laid out and had even picked out a costume for me. But that never worked out.

My role changed in 1984. I started by flying in a few samples, and one of the 'Changes' vocal samples. (sings 'Chang...ez'). And then Jon came up with this idea that he wanted a Vocoder [a voice synthesizer], and I knew a lot about them. After we got that, all hell broke loose. Jon kept giving me parts. He once gave me a part on a napkin that he'd written at lunch, just as we were about to go onstage and told me to 'play that'. I said 'Are you kidding? This is Yes! I gotta practice!' He had a lot of faith. It evolved from a few parts here and there to the point that I was playing in every song. I even got a Casio keyboard for the plane so Trevor [Rabin] and I could go over parts, but that was a mistake. Because I got a lot of parts handed to me! I was even doubling some of Trevor's guitar solos in places, like in 'It Can Happen'. The solos spots were the hardest part of playing offstage, and there were parts of 'Soon' [Anderson's solo piece] that we never got synched very well because we didn't have the eye co-ordination, so Tony took over those and I'd play the Vocoder.

In the same interview, Kevin Mulryne asked Casey if he regretted not being seen by the audience:

Well, in South America [in 1985] I was up on the side of the stage – you could see me from anywhere! But to get thrown in ten days before a major tour – with Yes – it took a load off that I could concentrate on my parts without having to worry about entertaining. It was a tough gig – I really had to concentrate. But everyone on that tour was always trying to make it better. Roy Clair would even fly out to make sure the sound system was right. Yes was a high-end client for Clair Brothers – it was a highly technical show reproducing a highly technical record. I even met Trevor Horn when they sent me over to Sarm studios to pick out yet more parts [from *90125*] for the European leg of the tour.

The tour was initially scheduled to begin at the end of January 1984 but received a setback when Rabin was accidentally injured while on holiday. He told *Rock Candy*:

Just before we were due to start rehearsals for the tour, my wife and I went on holiday to Miami. We were in the hotel swimming pool, and there was a water slide next to me that I hadn't really noticed. Suddenly a very large woman came hurtling down the slide and crashed straight into me. The collision was so bad that it ruptured my spleen and put me in hospital. I needed an operation and was out of action for a few weeks. We had no choice but to push all the dates back for a month or so while I recovered.

Initially scheduled to begin in Florida at the end of January, the tour was put back to begin on 28 February 1984 in Millersville, Pennsylvania. It continued through the spring into the middle of May in the USA and Canada, before an extensive jaunt round Europe, arriving in the UK mid-July for a somewhat spartan three gigs on home soil, two of which were at Wembley Arena, where I saw them. Another Summer jaunt around the USA in August and September led to a break of a couple of months. The tour finished in South America the following winter, which included two

nights playing to an astonishing 400 000 people, headlining at Rock in Rio. That the band should headline over the likes of Queen and AC/CD shows their stature at the time. In 1973 – as the *Close to The Edge* era gave way to *Tales From Topographic Oceans* - Yes were vying for 'biggest band in the world' stature. At the end of 1984, they were once again at the peak of their commercial powers.

It's worth dwelling on the shows for a moment. A typical set had the majority of *90125* being played (only 'Our Song' bit the dust, although it was played a few times) plus a few older pieces, mostly, unsurprisingly, from *The Yes Album*. 'And You And I' was also played mid-set, with 'Roundabout' the encore. The inevitable solo spots were also in evidence. At the time, White played a kit that mixed acoustic and electronic drums, and 'Leave It' – played as a showcase piece after 'Cinema' at the start of the set – had all five musicians singing (and a lot of vocal enhancements from Young) and White thumping two electronic pads from a different position onstage. Anderson played a little acoustic guitar and some inaudible keyboards during, for instance, Rabin's lengthy solo on 'City of Love'.

Access All Areas, Steven Soderberg's behind the scenes film, shot mainly in Hartford, Connecticut, is a fascinating watch. The band had their own jet – with logo painted on, and limo transportation, of course. There are a few Spinal Tap moments (especially Rabin complaining about the quality of a packing case), but it's the sheer mundanity of the backstage experience that comes across. Rabin shows himself to be the perfectionist even at that stage, wanting a Howe-esque 'build' into the closing section of 'Starship Trooper' that seemed to have been truncated as the tour wore on and Kaye comes across as laid back and affable.

The official video record, of course, is *9012:live*, a show from Edmonton in Canada in late September. Again, Soderberg was at the helm, and the video that was released in 1985 is a quirky, dated affair, offering only an hour of the show, and seemingly featuring as little as the band as possible, as it concentrates on found footage, presumably designed to show off the director's skills with 1980s video effects. It's far too busy, although the DVD (rarely available these days) does have a director's cut that features only the band. Another show at Dortmund in Germany was also filmed and can be seen on YouTube as a 45-minute cut, with the songs out of order. It's a bit rough and ready but offers a rather more authentic concert experience than the Soderberg film.

For the record, I have long held up my experience of seeing this version of Yes in July 1984 as one of my finest concert experiences – surpassing

Right: Despite some issues in the Asia camp at the time, Geoff Downes was still seen as an innovator in the world of new keyboards. Here he is on the cover of *Keyboard* magazine in November 1984. (*David Watkinson Collection*)

Left: A dapper Alan White photographed in *Modern Drummer* in 1985. (*David Watkinson Collection*)

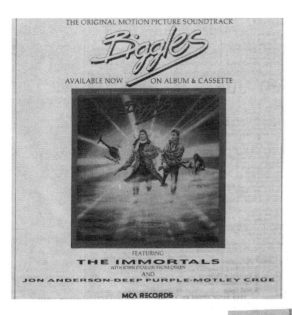

This page: During 1985 and 1986, Jon was only partially occupied in Yes as the band laboured on *Big Generator*. Here we see an advert for the *Biggles* movie, with contributions from Jon on the soundtrack. It was these recordings that David Watkinson witnessed being made when he visited Jon's studio as a result of the raffle he won (ticket pictured). He also took a quick snap of Jon driving away in his fashionable Jeep. (*David Watkinson Collection*)

99

even 1978 on the *Tormato* tour. Perhaps it was the presence of the youthful Rabin and his 'guitar hero' persona; perhaps it was the excitement of the success that *90125* brought. Perhaps it was the cartoons that opened the show. This was a very different Yes. But yet, there was enough of the old band to bring comfort. Whatever the reason, the shows were magnificent, and there was a genuine excitement in the auditorium that I can't remember from the many other Yes shows I've been to over the years.

For David Watkinson, a great fan of *90125*, the shows in 1984 were overwhelming:

I saw Yes three times as I always do when they tour, so that you minimise the chance that one gig might not work out well, not necessarily due to the band, but due to the hazards of an arena show: to someone chatting all the time; sound bouncing around or a big guy sitting in front of you.

The show can be summed up in one word, really: 'Wow'. From the Bugs Bunny cartoon start, the costumes, set list, power, energy, lighting, the band absolutely smashed it. What a tremendous feat of creativity and change for them. The songs were so fresh and lively, and the production of *90125* was impeccable. They just sounded like a Yes that's been through the wash and removed any stains from the previous decade – coming out all shiny and new.

I recall waiting outside Wembley Stadium to see the band and Jon waving at us; I loved the excitement when in the venue too. I was lucky to be seated in the special section of the area reserved for guests, family and friends. Behind me, I had Billy Connolly and Phil Collins, so obviously, I took the opportunity to speak to Phil. 'Phil – good to see you here. Do you like Yes then?' 'I have always liked them,' he replied 'I love the early days especially'.

The band put on a blinding show as always and the drop of lighting rig at the end of 'Starship Trooper' was a huge 'wow' moment for everyone. The 'Hello Goodbye' outro washed into my brain as I left the show, giddy with the effect that the band had on me.

All Change In Asia

At the start of 1984, John Wetton returned to Asia after discussions with Brian Lane and the other three members of the band. The foursome went to John Henry's rehearsal studio near Holloway (the same facility that Cinema / Yes had used two years earlier) to start rehearsing some of the material that was due to appear on the band's third album *Astra*. While

Howe thought that the old magic had returned, Wetton disagreed, citing musical differences (principally). Howe exited Asia at that point and, aside from the odd guest appearance, would not play with Wetton or Palmer for 25 years.

Although Downes remains the only constant in a career with Asia that continues to this day, we will part ways with the band at this point. *Astra* was finally released in 1985 on Geffen with former Krokus guitarist Mandy Meyer on guitar. Meyer is an excellent musician but plays in a much more conventional hard-rock style than Howe. The album was to be the band's last as a big-league hitmaking outfit, and following its relative failure, the band took seven years to release their next record (which included Howe as a guest, but not Wetton), by which time the world had completely changed.

Howe found some employment during the year via Trevor Horn, of all people, who by this time had launched ZTT records. Howe played on the Frankie Goes To Hollywood album *Welcome To The Pleasuredome*, but otherwise, it was transitional year for the guitarist. It was not to be the last of that sort in the 1980s for him.

Rick Wakeman – *Crimes of Pasion*

Personnel:
Rick Wakeman: keyboards, composition, production
Bimbo Acock: saxophones
Chas Cronk: bass
Maggie Bell: vocals
Rick Fenn: guitar
Tony Fernandez: drums & percussion
1. It's a Lovely Life 2. Eastern Shadows 3. Joanna 4. The Stretch 5. Policeman's Ball
6. Stax
7. Taken in Hand 8. Paradise Lost 9. The Box 10. Web of Love 11. Dangerous Woman

Rick wrote and performed the music to this bizarre thriller directed by his old friend Ken Russell. It was one of Russell's rare excursions into mainstream cinema, and it's no surprise that sexual themes are heavily featured. In it, a fashion designer played by Kathleen Turner – at the height of the 'sex kitten' phase of her career – becomes a prostitute by night, and all kinds of darkly erotic adventures ensue. It's not a classic. Rick's music – with 10CC guitarist Rick Fenn's guitar prominent throughout – stands up well on its own, although taken as an album, it feels a tad histrionic – just like the film itself. The one vocal track that appears in the film – 'It's A Lovely Life' – is actually very good – one of Rick's best, in fact, but is not helped by a rather over the top, piercing lead vocal by Maggie Bell.

1984 was a lean year for Rick, and to lend his talents to *Beyond the Planets* – produced by Sky guitarist Kevin Peek and Trevor Spencer – must be seen as a misstep. Produced for budget label Telstar as a mail-order cheap knock off of Jeff Wayne's mega-hit *The War of The Worlds*, the album is often credited to Peek, Wayne and Wakeman on digital services, but in fact, Wayne wrote only the overture, and Rick plays on three pieces, composing only the final section of the final track 'Beyond'. The majority of the album features synth-rendered reimaginings of Gustav Holst's *Planet Suite*. No doubt considered high tech at the time, these versions have dated badly. In short, this is horrible, but it's definitely not Rick's fault. To have short bursts of narration by Patrick Allen in what seems like a way of suggestion Richard Burton's narration on *War of The Worlds* is disconcerting, as his voice was so synonymous with the UK government's nuclear war warnings from the time, that it lends a sinister edge to the album. If reading this has tempted you to give the album a listen, I suggest otherwise.

1985 – Solo Shenanigans

9012Live: The Solos

Personnel:
Jon Anderson: lead vocals, acoustic guitar
Trevor Rabin: guitars, keyboards, vocals
Chris Squire: bass guitar, vocals
Tony Kaye: piano, Hammond organ
Alan White: drums
Yes: production
Paul Massey: engineer
Paul de Villiers: engineer, sounds
Released 7 November 1985
Highest chart places: UK: 44, USA: 81
Tracklisting: 1. Hold On (Rabin, Squire, Anderson) 2. Si (Kaye) 3. Solly's Beard (Rabin) 4. Soon (Anderson) 5. Changes (Rabin, Anderson, White) 6. Amazing Grace (Traditional, arr. Squire) 7. Whitefish (Squire, White)

Yes spent a lot of 1985 'resting' as a band, following the gruelling tour of 1984 that finished in the early months of 1985. Given that a new album was expected in 1986, and to maintain some of the momentum built during the year previously, Atco released something of an oddity – *9012live The Solos* – in November 1985.

Now almost forgotten as existing at all in the Yes 'canon', this folly contains just seven tracks. Buyers might have hoped for a full live album from the tour that millions experienced rather than the live VHS video that was released instead, but this album, in effect, acts as a companion to the video. Only two full-band tracks are included, both taken from the video soundtrack, in 'Hold On' and 'Changes'. These are both fine, but of course, the listener wants more. Tony Kaye's solo 'Si' is short and entertaining enough, built largely around Bach's 'Toccata and Fugue'. Rabin's jazzy 'Solly's Beard' – played on acoustic guitar with backing from Kaye (or possibly Young) – was the mainstay of his solo spots for many years. It sounds ok, though the technology wasn't really there in 1984 to make acoustic guitars, playing with that level of attack, sound really good. The audience enjoys the fast bit, but as a piece of music in isolation in its own right, it doesn't really work. Anderson gets a great crowd reaction to his keyboard-backed take on 'Soon' from *Relayer*. But again, it's short and exists only as a nostalgia trip for 'old school' Yes fans, rather than anything anyone buying the album would want to play more than once.

After 'Changes' on side two, the rest of the album is devoted to Squire and White. Squire begins with the bass and bass pedals sonic shock that is 'Amazing Grace', part of his solo since the *Drama* tour and seemingly designed to shatter vital organs throughout the audience. It segues into 'The Fish', with help from Rabin (in the same way that Howe had done previously), here called 'Whitefish' because of the solo sections given over to Alan White. Again, it's all well done (probably the best of the solo spots in terms of performance) and Squire references 'Tempus Fugit' with Anderson singing the 'Yes, Yes' section plus 'Ritual' from *Topographic Oceans*, but it's definitely a case of 'you had to be there'. I can't see anyone wanting to play this more than once – your author playing it for the 2nd time in his life to review it for this book.

A CD issue in 2009 added 'City of Love' and 'It Can Happen', but even with those two songs in place, it's hard to understand why the album was released, or indeed, what new Yes fans thought about all those solo spots when they saw the band live in the first place. Surely a full live album containing some vintage Yes classics, would have sold better, rather than this – frankly – throwaway offering?

Rick Wakeman – *Silent Nights*

Personnel:
Rick Wakeman: keyboards, vocals, lead vocal, composition, production
Tony Fernandez: drums, percussion
Chas Cronk: bass guitar
Rick Fenn: guitar
Bimbo Acock: saxophone
Gordon Neville: lead vocals
Recorded: October–December 1984 at Herne Place (Sunningdale, Berkshire) and Strawberry Hill (Dorking, Surrey)
Released 1985
Tracklisting: 1. Tell 'Em All You Know 2. The Opening Line 3. The Opera 4. Man's Best Friend 5. Glory Boys 6. Silent Nights 7. Ghost of a Rock 'n' Roll Star 8. The Dancer 9. Elgin Mansions 10. That's Who I Am

Rick Wakeman – *Live at Hammersmith*

Personnel:
Rick Wakeman: keyboards

Rick Fenn: guitars
Gordon Neville: lead vocals, percussion
Tony Fernandez: drums
Chas Cronk: bass
John Acock: mixing
Recorded: Hammersmith Odeon, London, May 9, 1985
Released 1985
Tracklisting: 1. Arthur 2. Three Wives 3. Journey 4. Merlin

Following the end of his contract with Charisma, Rick now had a new contract with President Records. President were – and remain – an indie label, but a prestigious one, whose main successes had come in the 1960s, but the relationship with President was to be a long term one for Rick. The label's business model was different to Charisma and A & M, and they did not expect massive chart success from their new signing. Budgets were lower, but so were expectations.

Silent Nights itself is very varied – probably too varied, if truth be told. Rick has described the album as 'confused', and that comes across in the choice of material. Aside from the unflushable Tony Fernandez, this new band was full of tried and tested professionals. Rick Fenn, once of 10CC (and a current member of that band as I write this) provided guitar, while Chaz Cronk (again, freshly out of The Strawbs, a band he's now a member of again) was on bass with vocals by versatile singer Gordon Neville, once of Scottish band Beggar's Opera. The confusion even extends to the cover, which is attractive but somewhat unrepresentative of the music within. It mixes hard rock with some poppier pieces – the rather lovely title track being one, which feels like a lost 10cc song, and the final salvo 'This Is Who I Am' which has the ring of The Who about it. However, with no Tim Rice to give lyrical structure, and Rick flexing his somewhat unreliable pen in that department once again, there's no real cohesion, with Rick attempting a couple of quirky tracks on side two, with 'Ghost Of A Rock 'n' Roll Star' and the cringe-worthy 'The Dancer'. That these are followed by a minor classic in the delightful instrumental 'Elgin Mansions' feels like something of a miracle.

Overall, it's not quite on a par with the underrated *Cost of Living*, but it does have its moments and contains some decent performances and songwriting. Indeed, it's this area that impresses the most, as Rick's playing is often marred by typically 1980s polysynth fanfares and trite lead patches. It's by no means a disaster, though.

Despite his inability to sell mass copies of his new albums, Rick was still popular enough in the mid-1980s to tour large theatres in the UK, and a tour in the spring of 1985 was followed by a US jaunt later in the year.

Silent Knights was considered a success, despite no chart placing, but *Live at Hammersmith*, the live album that came from the tour – with the same band that had recorded the album – displayed an early indication of the label's canny priorities, with the track selection taken entirely from Rick's 1970s albums. The versions are good, with Wakeman, as usual, displaying fine judgement in rearranging his own work. Gordon Neville struggles manfully with the vocals and Rick's keyboard sounds – mainly provided by Korg – are very much 'of their time' – lacking the character that his previous analogue instruments gave.

But Rick's best moment of 1985 was on neither album. Instead, it was his marvellously spirited them tune for *Lytton's Diary*. This was an ITV light drama series, produced by Thames TV and starring the suave Peter Bowles – a huge star in the UK at the time – as a press gossip columnist. In a short video piece in early 2021, Wakeman described how he was asked by Thames to write and perform one of two pieces – *Lytton's Dairy*, which ran for two six-part series (not one, as Rick suggests) or police drama *The Bill*. 'I think it's still going now', says grumpy old Rick of *The Bill*. He's not far off – it ended after 26 series in 2010, and drummer Charlie Morgan and bassist Andy Pask wrote the theme tune. No doubt Rick would have done a fine job as he did with *Lytton's Diary*, which was released as a single by President in 1985, but not released on an album. It's splendid.

Although all evidence of this seems to have been expunged from history, excepting a brief mention on a Sky band fansite, Rick – it seems – took part in an Australian tour with the band Sky as (amazingly) *second* keyboardist to Steve Gray in 1985. He makes no mention of it specifically in his autobiography, although, to be fair, he does concentrate on 'personal issues' and his religious beliefs particularly in that book. The dates of this tour are not recorded, but it's likely that it took place over the British summer (the Australian winter) during a gap between Rick's own UK tour and some US dates in August.

Your author does remember an appearance by the band – with Rick present – on the Val Doonican show sometime in June or July 1985. Doonican was a popular Irish crooner who had a light entertainment career throughout the 1960s, 70 and 80s on British TV. Sky had made two previous appearances on his show in 1979 and 1982, so it's logical to assume the Australian tour was after the TV appearance, although it may have been a little later in the year. Rick was interviewed alongside the rest of the band on the show and said something conciliatory, the implication being that he'd joined as a full-time member. He hadn't, of course. A solo Australian tour is also mentioned in Rick's autobiography, *Say Yes*.

Jon Anderson as a Gun for Hire

Let's step outside our fairly strict chronology for a moment to consider the 1980s career of Jon Anderson as a guest vocalist. Between 1983 and 1987, Anderson – alongside his solo career, his albums with Vangelis and, of course, Yes – was also available as a guest vocalist both for films and on the records of other artists. He had an advantage that his bandmates in Yes didn't have, of course, in that as the voice of 'Owner Of A Lonely Heart' – a number one hit in the USA – his role was very clearly defined. He was seen as a hitmaker for a while, and this led – in the short term at least – to some meaty opportunities.

The sequence of guest appearances began fairly modestly with a lead vocal on 'In High Places' from Mike Oldfield's 1983 album *Crises*. It's a very fine performance and was released as a single four years later in 1987, although it's hard to imagine this angular piece being a hit when 'Moonlight Shadow' is on the same album. It's a great track, though.

His first movie appearance was not a high profile one, recording two tracks with former Led Zeppelin bassist (and keyboard player) John Paul Jones on the soundtrack for the completely forgotten Michael Winner thriller *Scream for Help*. 'Christie' is a pleasant enough ballad, well suited to Jon, while 'Silver Train' is a slice of twangy, Duane Eddy-influenced rock and roll, which, if nothing else, demonstrates Jon's versatility.

However, he hit the big time, and by that, I mean the lucrative world of American movie soundtracks later in 1984. Firstly, he sang the Giorgio Moroder-penned 'Cage of Freedom' on the soundtrack to the revamped re-release of Fritz Lang's *Metropolis* – quite a high-profile release at the time. It's a plodding rock song and the melody is clearly not the sort that Anderson would normally sing, being better suited to a more conventional rock singers, until a final section after a bass solo, when he sounds more comfortable, but it's decent enough.

More suited to Anderson's voice, however, were his two 1985 appearances. 'This Time It Was Really Right' might be a mouthful of a song title, but it's a catchy 80s rock track on the soundtrack of the hit Brat Pack movie *St. Elmo's Fire*. John Parr had a big hit with the title song, of course, and it's one of the most impressive soundtrack albums of the era, filled – in the main – with the hard rock starts of the mid-1980s, including Bill Squier and Fee Waybill. Anderson doesn't sound out of place at all, and his song, written with Canadian composer David Foster (no relation to Anderson's former bandmate in The Warriors), might have been a hit single in a parallel universe.

Given his success with Vangelis, Anderson also seems beautifully suited to the lovely ballad 'Loved By the Sun', which appeared on the soundtrack to the Tom Cruise fantasy vehicle *Legend*. Indeed, his voice suits the swirling Tangerine Dream arrangement beautifully (it's as reminiscent of Vangelis as it is of the band's own music).

At this point, of course, as we shall see, Anderson was in something of a state of limbo and dipping in and out of the Yes set up. He was living in London while the rest of the band attempted to get to grips with the album in Italy and London. David Watkinson got up close and personal to Jon during 1985 as he recorded two tracks for the film *Biggles* in 1985 with Soviet composer Stanislas Syrewicz:

It was a sunny June day in 1985 in Brighton, on the south coast of England. A 24-year-old me and two friends had met up at a record fair in Brighton along the seafront. After that event, one of my mates drove us all over to Saltdean [a town close to Brighton]. A special fundraising open day at St. Aubyn's school would feature the grand draw and the potential to win one of the many prizes on offer. This – or perhaps Roedean – was thought to be the school Jon's daughter attended. I arranged the visit as there was only one prize I wanted and that was to meet Jon Anderson. It was not guaranteed that he would be there, but we thought that there was a slim chance, so we all went along and had a look at the celebrities that might turn up. I don't remember seeing anyone else as my blinkers were only set for Jon. We walked around the outside of the school and yes, I spied Jon at distance. We approached and met Jon and his daughter – they were all lovely.

Later in the day, I won the raffle! The prize was a visit to the studio with Jon. On the day, finding the studio in the pleasant area of London wasn't too bad and I was welcomed by the studio assistant. I was shown to a studio were Jon was and was shown around the mixing room. Jon was listening to his recording of his part in the movie *Biggles*. Much discussion was going on – some of it heated – with someone I presumed was the producer. I had not seen this sort of thing before, but it was all in aid of music, I guess.

I spoke with Jon again and as we finished both his business and my look around, Jon said goodbye and then asked, 'where are you going to', to which I replied that I was going to Victoria Station. Jon replied, 'ah...I'm going there to meet my daughter who is coming up from school; I'll take you – jump in the Jeep'.

My mind was blown again! I hopped into his Jeep and we merrily chatted all the way to Victoria Station; I headed to the platform with Jon, where we arrived just in time to greet Deborah, his daughter. I said hi and thanked Jon. Both days were pretty special occasions and ones that I'll never forget.

The *Biggles* film was a flop, albeit a high profile one, and it marks the end of Anderson as a contributor to movie soundtracks in the 1980s, as Yes, his solo career and ABWH became all-consuming. The two tracks on this soundtrack are exceedingly odd. 'Do You Want To Be A Hero' seems to want to be 'Owner Of A Lonely Heart' with its mannered 1980s affectations, while 'Chocks Away', awash with vocal effects, doesn't really work at all outside the context of the movie.

There were still a few more guest appearances with other artists as Jon shifted his attention to the USA before moving there permanently in the 1990s. In 1986, he snagged a video shoot in an exotic location for the excellent 'Shine' with Mike Oldfield again, which deserved to be a bigger hit, and around the time that he recorded *In The City of Angels* in Los Angeles, he made appearances as a backing vocalist on two 1987 releases. He appeared on the catchy song 'Moonlight Desires' on Canadian musician Laurence Gowan's album *Great Dirty World,* (a big hit in Canada) also making an appearance in the video with a heavily-mulleted Gowan. He also sang on 'Stop Loving You', a bona fide US hit for Toto from their album *The Seventh One.*

What can we learn from Anderson's excursions as a guest vocalist? First of all, while he's had undoubted success from time to time as a lead vocalist it's likely that he's considered an 'acquired taste' by the public at large. In an era of macho 'belters' in the style of John Parr, Anderson's distinctive alto no doubt delighted some but put off others. However, the last two tracks by Gowan and Toto show off Anderson's not inconsiderable worth as a backing vocalist. The skillfully mixed Toto song, in particular, really benefits from Jon's high register vocals within the vocal arrangement. Had he chosen to pursue it, he might have made a real living for himself as a specialist backing vocalist.

Jon Anderson – *Three Ships*

Personnel:

Jon Anderson: Lead Vocals

'Beyond War Philharmonic': orchestration, concert Master: Paul Cheng, conducted by Bob Esty

Gospel Choir: Calvary Baptist Church, Santa Monica

Inspirational Choir, courtesy of Pastor Robert de France Jr., Choir Director: William Bryant II

Children's Choir: 'Reach for the Stars Singers', Choir Director: Marta Woodhull

Sandra Crouch & Friends: Directed by Andre and Sandra Crouch & Gary Lanier

Sandra Crouch: special guest Duet Vocals on 'Oh Holy Night'

Jade Anderson: Additional Vocals on 'Jingle Bells'

Rhett 'Pepsi' Lawrence: Fairlight CMI,

Mike Marshall GB: Keyboards, orchestration

Trevor Rabin and Elliot Easton: Guitar

Frankie Banali & Ric Parnell: Drums & Percussion

Paulinho da Costa: Percussion

Novi Novog: Electric Viola

Produced by Roy Thomas Baker

Engineered & mixed by George Tutko

Recorded at Crystal Studios, Hollywood, CA.

Released December 1985

Highest chart places: USA: 166

Production Co-ordination by Bob Keasler, assisted by Freddie Henderson & Jem Scott

Musical Arrangements by Bob Esty except track 18, Mike Marshall GB

Tracklisting (1985 versions): 1. Save All Your Love 2. Easier Said Than Done 3. 3 Ships 4. Forest of Fire 5. Ding Dong! Merrily on High 6.Save All Your Love (Reprise) 7. The Holly and the Ivy 8. Day of Days 9. 2000 Years 10. Where Were You? 11. O Holy Night 12. How It Hits You 13. Jingle Bells

Back in 1985 specifically, while the rest of the band rested, Anderson not only continued his career as a guest vocalist, but used Yes' short rest period to record his fourth solo album. *Three Ships*, released at the back end of 1985 to tap into the Christmas market, is an odd beast. First of all, recorded in California rather than Europe, it sees Anderson experimenting with electronic textures rather than the prog rock of *Animation*. It sort of works, but the thumping electronic percussion has dated the album badly. What Anderson seems to be doing is taking his interest in keyboards – which he began to explore in earnest on *Animation* – and discard many of the rock elements to produce something that, with the benefit of hindsight, hasn't really stood the test of time.

Tonally, *Three Ships* is half a Christmas album, with some pleasant if lightweight renditions of Christmas pieces like 'O Holy Night' and 'Day of Days'. It's all disposable stuff, if truth be told, although there are a few interesting arrangements, and the rendition of the title track is unusually bold, combining the traditional song with rasping electronica.

The other half of the album is given over to other solo material that, while some of the lyrics could be called 'spiritual' and might even be linked to the Christmas spirit, really might have been on any Anderson solo album. Like *Animation*, there's a song written with Vangelis in 'Easier Said Than Done', and like 'Surrender', its counterpoint on the previous album, the track is as light as a feather, with its eye on the singles charts. Once again, it failed to make much of a mark. 'Forest of Fire' sees Anderson experimenting with ethnic textures, although the piece sounds like it's been plucked from a longer track.

However, there is bona fide Anderson classic on the album, even if we do have to wade through a lot of fluff to get to it, in the storming 'How It Hits You' which closes the record (except for a short coda, featuring Anderson's then four-year-old daughter Jade singing 'Jingle bells'). It's a beautifully constructed longer piece, with a terrific chorus and an exuberant vocal performance from Anderson, singing solo on an album where his voice is often double-tracked. The 'Ding Dong Merrily On High' breakdown towards the end links an otherwise ambiguous song back to the album's semi-concept. It's one for the ages on an otherwise disappointing record.

Anderson dedicated *Three Ships* to Beyond War, with Anderson wearing a branded jacket on the back cover. Beyond War were an international organization (although based in California) that mounted a campaign during the 1980s to end war. At the time of writing, its aims have not been met, sadly.

1986 - Italian and London Adventures

'Second album syndrome' is a fate that befalls many bands. Despite the general belief that this phenomenon occurs early in a band's life, it can, in fact, happen at many points in a group's career. It is often the case that it can occur a band goes through a major upheaval or a lineup change. Or perhaps a group or artist finds itself suddenly back in fashion with a hit on its hands, as was the case with this new version of Yes. If *90125* was the 'first' album, what of the second? The parallels with Asia are obvious. When Cinema formed at the start of 1982, it was a new band, developing new material over an extended period of time and then sifting out the less impressive songs as the process wore on. That Cinema morphed into Yes was both a happy quirk of fate and also a shrewd commercial move. But the pressure was on. As with all successful bands, the record company wanted a follow-up. 'More of the same, and while you're at it, lots of hits, please'.

With the final dates on the *90125* tour completed at the start of 1985, the band took an extended break. Some rested, some worked. Anderson stayed busy, producing *Three Ships* as we have already seen, and continuing his mercurial 'vocalist for hire' career.

The band finally convened in the second half of 1985 to work on the follow up, beginning with rehearsals in Los Angeles. The first studio chosen for the actual recording was the remarkable Lark Studio in Caramati, Italy, with Trevor Horn once again at the helm. The studio was placed in an old castle near the town, about ten miles from Milan and also not far from Cremona, the home of violin manufacture for 500 years. Opinions differ as to why that location was chosen. Chris Squire repeatedly stated in interviews that the studio was selected to save money, while Rabin has suggested that it was chosen – by Rabin himself – because a residential facility out in the countryside would help the band bond again as a unit, 'I thought it would be a good idea to go there so that we could be together concentrating on the next set of songs,' he told *Rock Candy* in 2020, adding, 'but I couldn't have been more wrong'. In 1987, he also gave *Guitar World* an idea of the approach the band were looking for before for before they convened for the recording:

Before we started, we thought a lot about *Abbey Road* [by The Beatles] as a model in the sense that If we come up with an idea, why pressure ourselves into making it a song? Just have it there. If you can't come up with the chorus. Don't throw it out because it's not a complete song and don't put a bad chorus around it. Just leave the chorus out. So, it evolved into an album with long songs ranging from four to nine and a half minutes.

Well, isn't that how progressive rock is made, Trevor? Essentially, Rabin is describing the process that Yes used to write their classic albums in the 1970s as if the band were reinventing the wheel with the creation of *Big Generator*.

Two issues within the band that needed sorting out that were never quite resolved – but which needed that resolution desperately – were still in play. Firstly, with Kaye now established in the band, he could not be sidestepped by Horn as he had been during the recording stage of *90125*. This does seem to have been resolved somehow, as Kaye's writing credits on *Big Generator* – his most extensive on any Yes album that he played on – testify.

The more important personnel issue was the role of Jon Anderson in the band. As we have seen from the testimony of Casey Young on the *90125* tour, Anderson re-established a dominant role in how the band was run musically as the tour progressed, making arrangement changes on the fly. By the time that work on *Big Generator* began, would he be able to resume the role he had held in the band up until around 1977? There's little doubt that he wanted that. However, the suggestion (largely from Rabin) was made that the band convene as a four-piece first in Italy to work on the music. Anderson would arrive a little later to work on his vocals. So that put Anderson in his place, then. 'You're the singer, Jon – just write some lyrics and sing!'

Finding this 'a little odd', Anderson left the band to it for about six weeks, and when he arrived, he didn't like what he saw, as he told *Rock Candy* in 2020:

Some of the band wee partying way too much… and that created a terrible atmosphere. It didn't feel like the right environment for recording an album. Nothing much was happening, workwise, and nobody seemed that bothered about it. It was pretty dreadful.

In typically left-field style, Anderson had some ideas to lighten the mood. Jon in *Rock Candy* again:

I had a plan to use this huge room in the castle that had a stage in it. My idea was to bring in some musicians and acrobats from Milan that could perform in there and who could contribute to creating the right creative atmosphere. But Trevor [Horn] really didn't like the idea.

A good producer would have understood that the atmosphere was wrong. But that's what happens when you let someone from outside the band dictate how things were done. It was Trevor's job to make sure that we had the right atmosphere to encourage creativity, but he wasn't doing it – and that meant that we wasted loads of time and money at the studio in Italy. I think that if I'd been encouraged to get more involved in *Big Generator* from the start, and hadn't been kept so much at arm's length, then I could have made a difference and stopped some of what ended up happening.

Jon probably has a point, although it's not surprising that his rather 'out there' solution to the problem wasn't adopted, given his track record – remember cut out cows and bales of hay in the studio for the recording of *Tales From Topographic Oceans,* anyone?

In the end, the backing tracks were constructed and very little else was done. Squire had a different perspective, telling Malcolm Dome in 2010 that: 'My recollection is that we were too caught up in getting the right recording equipment installed, and that was more important than the music.' Rabin, however, told the same writer that he felt that Squire was simply trying to find an excuse for why so little got done.

Most likely, as in all things, it was a little bit of everything. In the end, it's quite possible that given the 'proclivities' of some of its members, that the band was ungovernable and unproducible at this point. They headed back to London, where Horn would be on much more familiar territory.

Back in the UK, however, things didn't improve. The band split into warring factions, with Horn in the middle. It is likely that family life also got in the way. Squire, in particular, was going through a marriage break-up. The band spent week after week in various studios across London – specifically Horn's own Sarm East and West studios and George Martin's Air Studios. The bills for the much-in-demand (by this time) Sarm East studios being generated by Horn's wife Jill Sinclair were eye-wateringly high, and very little progress was being made.

After a few months, Horn jumped ship, labelling the album 'unfinishable'. This was Squire's perspective, as reported to Malcolm Dome in 2010:

He couldn't deal with the way things weren't moving along at any sort of pace, plus he was having disagreements with Tony and Jon [no surprise there]. Which never helped anyone's mood. I was sorry to see him go, but looking back, it was for the best.

It's fairly clear that the sort of producer that Horn was – and which had worked so well when the band were creating *90125* – was not really what was required with this new album. Tony Kaye – in a rare interview – told Roy Trakin of *Rock Express*:

Legally, he had to get that credit, but in reality, this album was taken out of his hands pretty early on because he wasn't in tune with what we wanted. I believe the musicians should be the most important people in the project, not the producer. Trevor Horn didn't know how to cope with five individuals who had strict ideas about what the music should sound like.

Rabin took control. It's likely that most of the final album was 'in the can' by the time the band left London, but putting the pieces together was the key. With the permission of the rest of the band – but most importantly Anderson and Squire – Rabin enlisted the help of the band's live sound engineer Paul De Villiers and took the tapes to Los Angeles, where they set about a nine-week mixing process. Squire and Anderson were also on hand. Slightly bizarrely, given the shaky nature of their relationship, they rented a house together in the Los Angeles area, should they be needed. Anderson reports that while he continued to work on his project based around the life of artist Paul Chagall (still unreleased, at time of writing) and started to work on his *In the City Of Angels* album, Squire continued to indulge his rather more worldly impulses.

While this was – understandably – a time of high pressure for Rabin, given that he felt the need to justify the huge amount of time and cash spent on the album, but by the end of this process, in the first half of 1987, the band had an album.

GTR – *GTR*

Personnel:
Max Bacon: lead vocals
Steve Hackett: acoustic & electric guitars, guitar synthesizer, backing vocals
Steve Howe: acoustic & electric guitars, guitar synthesizer, backing vocals
Phil Spalding: bass guitar, backing vocals
Jonathan Mover: drums, percussion

Geoff Downes: producer, keyboards
Alan Douglas: engineer
Recorded at the Townhouse, London, 1985-86
Released July 1986
Highest chart places: UK: 41, USA: 11
Tracklisting (1986 version): 1. When the Heart Rules the Mind (Hackett, Howe), 2. The Hunter (Geoff Downes) 3. Here I Wait (Hackett, Howe) 4. Sketches in the Sun (Howe) 5. Jekyll and Hyde (Bacon, Hackett, Howe) 6. You Can Still Get Through (Hackett, Howe) 7. Reach Out (Never Say No) (Hackett, Howe, Spalding) 8. Toe the Line (Hackett, Howe) 9. Hackett to Bits (Hackett) 10. Imagining (Hackett, Howe, Mover)

It was 1985. Steve Howe was without a band having been ousted from Asia, while – across the progressive divide – Steve Hackett, previously of Genesis and participant in a rapidly collapsing solo career (caused, I might add, by fashion rather than a significant drop in quality in his own music) was also looking for a boost. The catalyst? Brian Lane, of course, who was still Howe's manager. He persuaded the two of them to get together and write, with a view to creating an album – and then perhaps a tour. In Lane's mind, this was the opportunity to create another supergroup to rival Asia. What could possibly go wrong?

Now, if in the unlikely event that you're reading about this project for the first time, you might think to yourself: 'That seems a bit contrived' – and you'd be right. Yet to both principals and Lane, it's not hard to see how appealing the project might be, and with both careers in the doldrums, why not give it a go?

The Geffen label had originally been interested via John Kalodner, but after blowing hot and cold for a while, it was Arista that finally took the project on. In his autobiography, Howe reports some confusion over this at the time, with Geffen financing some rehearsal space but Clive Davies at Arista suggesting a Geoff Downes song 'The Hunter' for the band, his interest getting the label the final nod. Tonally, as well as their own guitar stylings, the decision was made – particularly because of Hackett's interest in making the most of the new midi technology – to use guitar-controlled synths to create most of the keyboard-style sounds. Where those sounds could not be created comfortably in that way, Geoff Downes – who also produced – played keyboards.

As for the rest of the band, they were brought in very much as 'guns for hire'. Drummer Jonathan Mover was a British-based American who had been part of early sessions for the Marillion album *Fugazi* before being replaced by Ian Moseley. Bassist Phil Spalding was a session player, still known for being part of the Mike Oldfield extended musical family, while vocalist Max Bacon was best known for spells in hard rock bands Bronz and Nightwish, both of which had had some minor success but had not broken through commercially. Bacon was the crucial appointment since his high-register, AOR-style vocals would inform the music as much as the performance of the two band leaders, who, initially at least, were very much the bosses. This sort of 'manufactured band' approach was not the best way to create a new, living, breathing, touring unit.

However, the basic premise of the project was sound, in that the two guitarists planned to, as Alan Hewitt, Hackett's official biographer, says, 'facilitate the two guitarist's explorations of the entire of the entire range of options available via their chosen instrument.' Howe told Hewitt:

It was during the best phase of rehearsals which happened early in the first three months of 1985. We used to send the guys out and the two of us would work out guitar parts. That was when we formulated the basic parts for what we did on the album. There are lots of things that change in the studio. That was when we started getting the idea that we could work out. We thought that the two guitars were complimentary. I like working closely with one other person and that was the original flame. I suppose we were helping each other's songwriting, and by doing that, we were able to feature each other's guitar playing. It was really a question of developing new sounds. It was an exchange of ideas and techniques.

The corporate nature of the project was hinted at from the word go. Mover told Hewitt:

Actually, Phil Spalding and I had quite a bit of input with regard to the writing. But since we were the new guys along with Max Bacon, we were told that we would receive writing and publishing credits on one song apiece. One song became the one I had most input into, and that was 'Imagining'. But I also, along with Phil, had a lot to do with 'Here I Wait', 'Jekyll and Hyde', 'You Can Still Get Through' and 'Reach Out, Never Say No'.

Recording, under Downes' supervision, began at Townhouse Studios in London, the same facility at which Yes had recorded *Drama*. A symptom of the times was the amount of technology available, Howe reporting on the amount of technical experimentation employed in the studio, with 'individual reverb units, compressors and noise gates strapped across every sound source imaginable'. None more 80s. All this technology, plus the commercial expectations heaped on the project, moved the music in the direction of stadium rock.

If Howe is implying that the obsession with the technology at the time affected the sonics of the eventual album, which he probably is, then he's bang on the money. *GTR* – the album – has many merits and is well worth revisiting. But, sadly, it's one of the two worst *sounding* records of Howe's career, alongside the second Asia album, *Alpha,* although for entirely different reasons, as already discussed in the 1983 chapter. Partly because of the highly stylized 1980s sonics and partly because of the way that the arrangements have to work within some conventional AOR songwriting, the album also makes the rookie error of sometimes making two of the most distinctive and innovative guitarists of the era sound like each other. In short, it arguably bungled its main selling point. Furthermore, while the use of guitar synthesizers may have been innovative in itself, the end results are generic and a bit pointless. They may as well have been played by a keyboardist, as they were in a live setting, by Matt Clifford.

The hired guns actually acquit themselves well, with Phil Spalding in particular, getting a few moments in the spotlight and making the most of them. Mover is solid, although any subtleties in his playing tend to be buried in the GTR wall of sound, while Max Bacon delivers a full-on performance, singing at 'eleven' for almost the entire album (although for 'Toe the Line' he ratchets his voice down to about an eight). As a performance, it lacks intimacy, but then again, so does the album.

The album itself offers eight original songs, plus a solo piece for each of its two stars – one on each side – with Howe's 'Sketches in The Sun' one of his most memorable pieces outside the Yes cannon, although his choice of his faithful Steinberger guitar to play it on gives the piece a bright, piercing tone – there's certainly an argument that an acoustic version might have been more effective. 'Hackett To Bits' is actually a complex little ditty, drawing on Hackett's famous solo track 'Please Don't Touch' but throwing in several other elements, including a brief burst of Hackett's trademark Segovia-inspired Spanish guitar.

The album opens with the US hit 'When the Heart Rules The Mind'. It's a decent song in the AOR style so beloved of the US charts at the time, certainly, although it's on this track that the two guitarists sound most homogenized, and the mix has them booming when then should probably crunch. Bacon's voice is perfect for the song, though, and the backing vocals are effective if a little buried in the wall of sound mix. A little acoustic interlude also hits that the album isn't going to be *all* bombast. Downes' 'The Hunter' is another tuneful piece that loses itself in such a reverb-heavy mix that parts become difficult to discern. 'Here I Wait' teases with some Koto-stye sounds, before hitting us with a big, obvious riff, although the second half of the song does offer a slightly more ambitious instrumental excursion, even if most of the guitar lines do sound like they were recorded in a warehouse. 'Jeckyl and Hyde' – closing side one – is, for my money, the most successful track on the album, benefitting on a typically melodic lead melody from Hackett and a passage in which not only do the two guitarists duel, but they actually sound like themselves. For hints of what this contrived project might have achieved, look no further than this track.

Side two opens with 'You Can Still get Through', which is typical 1980s AOR, awash with big synth chords, but is impressive for all that, benefitting from some interesting guitar textures. It's another decent song, with both guitarists again soloing and Howe particularly good, while Spalding is allowed to stretch out in the song's coda. GTR have another go at heavy rock with only partial success on 'Reach Out (Never Say No)'. 'Toe The Line' is a pleasant and well-constructed ballad with a lovely Howe-penned acoustic intro, although it does build into power ballad territory, even if the final moments allow him to crank out the pedal steel to good effect. A big finish is called for, and we almost get it, with 'Imagining' and Hackett's beautiful Spanish guitar introduction, although the song itself disappoints, despite an imaginative, ascending riff and some excellent playing, especially from Howe.

Released in July 1986, the album performed creditably, particularly in the USA, where it reached number 11. A tour followed, beginning just before release, firstly in the USA and then Europe, finishing in September. The set included some songs by their previous bands as well as the entire album and a new song, 'Prizefighters'. However, all was not well by the time that the band started to think about their second album. It seems that the two main protagonists had a different perception of what the band was, and the usual managerial and financial issues pushed a wedge between them. Everyone – management and label specifically – expected the band to be the new Asia, but they hadn't reached the required level of success. Eventually, Hackett had had enough and left the project, as did Mover, who had been biding his time after disliking the way his drum parts had been treated on the album and had moved back to the USA.

There were two further phases of the struggling band after Hackett's departure. With Howe as the only guitarist but with Bacon and Spalding on board, the band recorded some demos, but the label decided not to pick up the band in that incarnation. Some of this material has appeared for the first time on Howe's *Anthology 2,* released in 2017, with Bacon's singing. To these ears, the tracks are decent and well performed but lacking in real distinctiveness.

However, Arista did finally approve another member – if not a like-for-like replacement – in American Robert Berry. A new phase of recording took place with the support of the label. Howe mentions that this might have been a new project rather than GTR; a logical view, since Berry was a multi-instrumentalist and songwriter rather than a guitarist with a distinctive style, and his instrumental role in the band was as rhythm guitarist. The group tried some of Berry's material, although Bacon was wary of Berry's ambitions to sing lead. However, out of the blue, in the middle of recording, Berry left to join Carl Palmer and Keith Emerson in the ill-feted '3' project. GTR (or Nero and the Trend as they were playfully calling themselves) fell apart in financial chaos.

A bootleg version of a possible second album does circulate but should be treated with extreme caution. However, one track from these sessions (and not on the bootleg) has been released officially – twice! The song 'No One Else To Blame', which is exceptionally good – has been issued on Max Bacon's solo album *The Higher You Climb* (where his version features guitar from Steve Howe) and on Robert Berry's *Pilgrimage to a Point,* both released during the 1990s.

1987 was to be yet another transitional year for Steve.

Rick Wakeman – *Country Airs*

Personnel:
Rick Wakeman: piano, composition, production
Released: 1986
1. Dandelion Dreams 2. Stepping Stones 3. Ducks and Drakes 4. Morning Haze 5. Waterfalls 6. Quiet Valleys 7. Nature Trails 8. Heather Carpets 9. Lakeland Walks 10. Wild Moors

While it had its roots in the ambient music of the late 60s and early 1970s, by the mid-1980s, 'New Age' music had become big business in its own right, with labels like Wyndham Hill becoming huge organisations pedaling music that was specifically intended for relaxation and atmosphere. By the time that Rick came to write and perform *Country Airs,* British label Coda were becoming one of the best-known exponents of this sort of music, picking up artists like Claire Hamill (whose *Voices* album was recorded using only her multi-tracked vocals), *Tubular Bells* producer Tom Newman and Jon Anderson sideman, sax player Jim Morrissey. In 1986, Rick's financial woes had not lifted, and when offered £5000 by Coda to record a solo piano album of new material, he wrote ten new pieces based on his emotional responses to some country walks, recorded them for £2000 and paid off some important debts with the profits.

In an era of unfortunate cover designs, it's worth mentioning this one because it's atypical for Rick – a stylish white cover with a country scene inset – but very typical of the genre into which it was placed. Intending to evoke peaceful emotions, the album does just that. It's missing, as you might expect, many particularly memorable melodies, although some, like 'Waterfalls' obliquely evoke past tunes. There's nothing we haven't heard before in other pieces, but it's beautifully played and recorded and definitely 'does what it says on the tin'. If you like listening to Chopin for relaxation, you'll probably enjoy this. It was successful for the label and was the first of several such albums to be recorded by Rick over the next few years.

1987 – The Big Generator Finally Grinds into Action

Big Generator

Personnel:

Jon Anderson: vocals

Chris Squire: bass, vocals

Trevor Rabin: guitar, keyboards, vocals, string arrangements

Alan White: drums, percussion, vocals

Tony Kaye: Hammond organ and piano

James Zavala: horns on 'Almost Like Love', harmonica on Love Will Find a Way

Lee R. Thornburg: horns on 'Almost Like Love'

Nick Lane : horns on 'Almost Like Love'

Greg Smith: horns on 'Almost Like Love'

Produced by Yes, Trevor Horn, Trevor Rabin, Paul De Villiers

Recorded at Lark Studios, Italy; Sarm and Air studios, London and Southcombe, Westlake and Sunset Sound studios, Los Angeles between 1985 and 1987.

Released September 1987

Highest Chart Positions: UK: 17, USA: 15

1. Rhythm of Love (Kaye/Rabin/Anderson/Squire) 2. Big Generator (Rabin/Kaye/ Anderson/ Squire/White) 3. Shoot High Aim Low (White/Kaye/Rabin/Anderson/Squire) 4. Almost Like Love (Kaye/Rabin/Anderson/Squire) 5. Love Will Find a Way (Rabin) 6. Final Eyes (Rabin/Kaye/Anderson/Squire) 7. I'm Running (Rabin/Squire/Anderson/ Kaye/White) 8. Holy Lamb (Song for Harmonic Convergence) (Anderson)

And so, to the album that had caused so much stress over the past couple of years between 1985 and 1987. It's important, first off, to congratulate Trevor Rabin on the work he did pulling the album together to make it not only releasable, but as good as it is. I also realise that for some Yes fans, this whole era of Yes music was a betrayal of all that the band had achieved in the 1970s. The first thing to do must be to compare the album for its illustrious and best-selling predecessor *90125*. There's little doubt that – by a mixture of talent and good fortune – *90125* turned out to be an excellent album. Despite some of its modernist bells and whistles, it has stood the test of time exceptionally well. Horn's production is powerful yet intimate when it needs to be. However, the problem with *Big Generator* is – like many a failing relationship – that it lacks intimacy and, despite 'Almost Like Love's' Motown influences, it lacks soul.

There are two reasons for this. Firstly, the material is not quite up to scratch, despite some moments which – on the face of it – hint rather more at 'old' Yes than is evident on *90125*. But compare, if you will, 'And You And I' to 'Final Eyes'. On the former, the listener feels involved with the music – as if we are in the studio with Steve Howe as he says 'ok'. 'Final Eyes' sounds like it's played on a good sound system but 100 yards away. There's little doubting the craft and talent that has gone into the creation of *Big Generator*, and this is represented by some great playing and some stunning melodies, but the whole doesn't match the sum of its parts.

One wonders what Atco's expectations were when the album finally saw the light of day in September 1987. Certainly, it was a success by any standards except the sales of *90125*. It performed similarly in terms of chart placings in the USA and the UK, reaching 15 and 17 respectively. It reached platinum status in the USA, matching the performance of *Close To The Edge* (for instance), but a long way from the triple Platinum of *90125*. The label can't have been thrilled.

Were times a-changing? Had the release environment changed? Well, up to a point. The 1980s were a turbulent decade and styles moved on quickly. However, a look at the biggest successes of that year show that 'old man' rock music could still be successful, with *1987* by Whitesnake, *Hysteria* by Def Leppard and – most crucially – Pink Floyd's comeback album *A Momentary Lapse Of Reason*, released the same week as the Yes album, all big successes. Certainly, the two singles taken from the album – in 'Love Will Find A Way' and 'The Rhythm Of Love' did not offer anything like the innovation or the distinctiveness of 'Owner' either. The use of the word 'love' in both song titles is a coincidence but demonstrates a shift in power away from Horn's innovative sonic techniques towards Rabin's rather more cliché-ridden lyrical influences and rock-guitar impulses. While performing well in the US rock charts, they failed to enter the public consciousness with much degree of success, peaking at 30 and 40 in the USA, respectively.

No coincidence will be the similarity of the cover design to the template set out by *90125* – all computer graphics and BIG LETTERING. The original vinyl version was an attractive green and purple, the CD version (it was the first Yes album to get a quick CD release) a less attractive but more eye-catching yellow and pink.

Reviews were mixed, including from the band itself. Rabin told *Rock Candy*:

Big Generator will always be a disappointment for me. There are a few songs, such as the singles, which do work very well. But I listen to a lot of that material now and feel that it should never have been included. We made the mistake of letting a lot of tracks meander along when they really needed to be tightened up.

Anderson has similar feelings, also telling *Rock Candy:*

The album is no more than OK. There's still a lot of material on *Big Generator* that isn't up to the standards demanded of a Yes album. I listen back to it now and it feels like a bit of an anti-climax. After what we'd done with *90125*, *Big Generator* feels like coming back down to earth with a bump.

But do we agree? A strength of the album is the way it is sequenced over two sides of vinyl. Side one is almost perfect in this respect, while side two is where Rabin's meandering tracks enter the fray, but they work sequenced together if they work anywhere.

It's possible that 'Rhythm of Love' is the least sophisticated song in the Yes canon. Who'd have thought that Yes would write a song about sex with some very basic metaphorical content? It's not exactly down and dirty, but it does rock out quite hard. Not that there aren't plenty of subtleties to enjoy. The songs begins with some orchestral tones, followed by some beautifully-rendered Beach Boy-style harmonies, which persist throughout. Rabin – who varies his guitar tone expertly throughout the album – is relatively restrained, while Anderson sounds completely committed. Horn stabs recall 'Owner' without doing so in an in-your-face way, while White's drumming feels powerful and unforced; his snare sound gratifyingly natural for the times. Additionally, if *Big Generator* does anything better than its predecessor, it's in highlighting the strengths of the band's three main vocalists without contrivance, and Rabin and Squire also get short leads here, although it's Rabin that is most prominent in the backing vocals. His 'tapped' solo feels a touch OTT for the song, but overall it's storming opener – catchy, and beautifully produced, and fully deserving of the longevity it has been afforded.

Rabin cranks up the overdrive for the title track. This is as heavy as the album gets after an opening that again recalls a track from *90125*, this time 'Leave It'. There's some pleasing tension in the minor key verse, while the chorus offers some unusual vocal textures as well as those ubiquitous stabs of horn, not to mention a simulated horn section. It's hard to deny that this is another strong track within the context of the album, even throwing in a King Crimson-style guitar solo and a middle eight straight out of *L*-era Godley and Crème. This is thrilling modern guitar rock, even if Squire does sound like he's playing a Wal bass at times – no Rickenbacker, here!

'Shoot High, Aim Low' brings the pace down a little, with lyrics about the Nicaraguan conflict of the 1980s. It's hugely atmospheric and one of the better examples of the band seeming like they are in harmony. White's simple and insistent drum pattern, which anchors the song, was recorded in Italy, using the natural reverb of a room in the castle. It works beautifully and the song – with Anderson and Rabin playing different 'characters' – is fabulous. There is, however, an argument that says it's too long, meandering towards its fadeout with repetitions of lines from earlier in the song.

Squire wrote the horn riff for 'Almost Like Love' and stuck with his love of the track despite some discouragement from members of the band. Yes fans, over the years, have screamed 'sacrilege' at the use of a 'real' horn section on this song, but in reality, it doesn't sound much different to the imitation one used earlier on the album. Perhaps it's the Motown inspired drum pattern, or Rabin's chunky, jazz guitar or Anderson's half-sung, half-rapped verses. It just seems to leave some Yes fans feeling uncomfortable in a rather unhealthy way. Anyway, the song itself is tuneful and light as a feather, with no depth whatsoever, but as a piece of good-time rock and soul to close side one, it's very decent. Rabin hates it and has said so quite a lot. His solo is terrific, though, and Kaye gets to play some rasping Hammond.

Side two is where the wheels come off a bit, though it starts well enough with the rather splendid lead single 'Love Will Find A Way'. It's simply a good pop song; slated to be recorded by Steve Nicks until White heard it and suggested it for Yes. The string quartet that opens the track is a nice touch. Thereafter, it's built around two light Rabin riffs, and some stabbing polysynth. The first verse is sung in unison by all the vocalists, with Rabin singing solo on the chorus and the second vocalist. Anderson is demoted to 2nd lead, 'Changes' style. But the song really works, and while it might have been a bigger hit (30 in the USA, a lowly but hardly surprising 73 in the UK), it's glorious.

'Final Eyes' and 'I'm Running' both have issues, so we'll deal with them together. The songs provide a somewhat wonky backbone to side two. The former was extensively restructured by Rabin at the mixing stage, and it still lacks something – perhaps another idea or section – to make it work. The opening section, with Anderson singing over Rabin's acoustic guitar, should be an album highlight, but fails to work due to Rabin's overwrought production. It should sound intimate, but instead, it's distant and uninvolving – there's too much going on, although Squire's harmony vocals are delightful, and Kaye's Hammond hints at past glories. The song is so close to being great that it's frustrating. In the end, there's too much repetition, which is also a fault of 'I'm Running' (recorded during the London sessions), which again begins well, based around a Latin-inspired and extremely complex bass and acoustic guitar riff (written by Squire) and some brooding percussion from White. However, once again, there's too much repetition, and even though Rabin tries to pull it all together, the mixture of uninvolving production and repetitious arrangement leaves the listener frustrated. The result is a fundamentally decent track but a missed opportunity. Definitely another one for the 'what might have been' pile.

And so, to the final track, at which point the wheel that had been threatening to come off spin away in all directions. The album finishes on 'Holy Lamb', an Anderson song best relegated to the bonus tracks on a solo album. He sounds committed, but the arrangement is cursory at best. It's mercifully short, but given how important final tracks can be to a listener, it's a huge disappointment.

Big Generator is a very frustrating album. Its best moments are also some of its least 'Yes-like', but considering the near-chaos of its recording, it's amazing that it turned out as well as it did, for which Trevor Rabin must take a huge amount of credit.

Rick Wakeman – *The Family Album*

Personnel:
Rick Wakeman: keyboards, composition, production
Released: 1988
Tracklisting: 1. Black Beauty (black rabbit) 2. Adam (Rick's 2nd son) 3. Jemma (Rick & Nina's daughter) 4. Benjamin (Rick's 3rd son) 5. Oscar (Rick & Nina's son) 6. Oliver (Rick's 1st son) 7. Nina (Rick's wife) 8. Wiggles (black & white rabbit) 9. Chloe (German Shepherd) 3.59 10. Kookie (Cat) 11. Tilly (Golden Retriever) 12. Mum 13. Dad 14. The Day After The Fair 15. Mackintosh

Rick Wakeman – *The Gospels*

Personnel:
Rick Wakeman: keyboards, composition, production
Ramon Remedios: Tenor
Robert Powell: narration

The Eton College Chapel Choir: choir
Released: 1988
Highest chart place: UK: 94
Tracklisting: 1. St Matthew - The Baptism 2. St Matthew - The Welcoming   3. St Matthew - The Sermon on the Mount 4. St Matthew - The Lord's Prayer 5. St Mark - The Way 6. St Mark - The Road to Jerusalem 7. St Mark - Trial and Error 8. St Mark – Galilee 9. St Luke - The Gift 10. St Luke - The Magnificat 11. St Luke - Welcome a Star 12. St Luke – Power 13. St John - The Word 14. St John - The Hour 15. St John - The Children of Mine 16. St John - The Last Verse

The 1980s for Rick were all about the attempt to regain past glories that were after dashed, either by financial mismanagement (not necessarily his) or by indifference from the general public. It saw a gentle drift towards 'genre' music, his only salvation in the decade. *The Family Album* was his second 'new age' effort. It's a musical summary of his home life at the time, featuring musical portraits of Nina Carter and all his children, his mother and father and a fair few domestic pets. Despite many a floaty, gentle synth passage – Rick here uses some tinkling patches and even the piano passages have a sheen over them that almost demands 'relaxation'.

However, it doesn't really do the job as a new age album since moments of serenity are then followed by 'Merlin the Magician'—style honky-tonk craziness. After all, if Rick was going to create musical portraits of his family, he was hardly going to make them *all* awash with serenity. As a result, despite some good tunes, the album falls between a lot of stools. As for Rick, he understandably can't listen to it following the break up of his marriage to Nina, saying on his website:

An album that I can't play now as it is full of so much sadness for me. When it was first recorded, it was all about everybody in my family and life that meant everything to me. Now, many have passed on or have proven not to be the great loves I believed them to be at the time. Knowing what I know now, I would never have made this album.

A great deal of time during 1986 and 1987 was devoted to getting *The Time Machine* project off the ground, which was initially commissioned by major label Polydor. However, out of the blue came the opportunity to record something with a very different tone. Rick's local vicar, Graham Long, who had officiated at his marriage to Nina, offered him the opportunity to create a piece using the local church organ, based around the scriptures. Rick created an epic double album called *The Gospels,* featuring his keyboards, the choir of Eton College, narrator Robert Powell and well-known tenor Ramon Remedios.

Recorded on an eight-track machine on the same boat on the Thames that Rick had been using to record *The Time Machine,* the sonic quality of the album, as Rick correctly points out, is not the best, and the music suffers as a result, his keyboards failing to suggest the grandiosity required for the project. But, given that it's a long way from being a rock album, instead tailored for the Christian community, it's not a bad listening experience at all.

The album was released by Stylus records as another mail-order album to be advertised on TV, and as a result made a brief appearance in the UK chart, at number 94 in May 1987. It wasn't the end of the life of the music, and Rick was later able to revise it for a concert in Israel following an initial performance at the Royal Albert Hall in London.

This page: The success of *90125,* combined with its perceived level of sonic innovation, led to a lot of interest from the music press, particularly the technical rags. The whole band are featured in *Electronic Soundmaker,* while Tony Kaye is featured in *Keyboard,* both in mid-1984. *(David Watkinson Collection)*

ELECTRONIC
MAY 1984 75p
SOUNDMAKER
& C·O·M·P·U·T·E·R · M·U·S·I·C

YES
INTERVIEW

Super Prize Competition
WIN
A DAY IN THE STUDIO
WITH AN EMULATOR

1984
SYNTHESIZER
GLOSSARY

Atlantic Crossing

KEYBOARD

JUL '84

TONY KAYE
The Continuing Odyssey of YES

STEVE NIEVE

MAL WALDRON

ANDRE-MICHEL SCHUB

HOW TO
TRANSCRIBE SOLOS

EQUIPMENT REVIEWS:
DECILLIONIX DX-1
DIGI-ATOM 4800

WIN 100 FREE
ECM RECORDS

US $2.00
Canada $2.50
UK £1.35

This page: Live at Wembley, London, in 1984. The Yes show in 1984 was a massive production, from the stage set to the costumes and an innovative, descending lighting rig. The band seem to be relishing the show as well. (*David Watkinson Collection*)

This page: More shots from Wembley in 1984. As well as the five members of the band, the sound was enhanced by Casey Young, a second keyboard player positioned underneath the stage. His role grew as the tour went on so that by the time of the European shows, he was playing on every song. (*David Watkinson Collection*)

This page: Another selection from Wembley in 1984. This selection particularly demonstrates the showmanship on display from such an experienced selection of players. Chris Squire was the master of onstage charisma, while both Rabin and Kaye played with plenty of rock n roll style. (*David Watkinson Collection*)

This page: A final selection from the Wembley shows in 1984. Both of your authors attended these shows, although we didn't meet for another 35 years! We both remember the shows as amongst the best live experiences of our lives. (*David Watkinson Collection*)

Left: Into 1985 and the odd stop-gap release, *9012 Live – The Solos,* perhaps a full live album would have been a more appropriate souvenir of the tour. *(Atco)*

Right: Another technical magazine appearance – this time for Alan White in *Modern Drummer* in 1985. (*David Watkinson Collection*)

Left: Jon's 1985 solo album *Three Ships*. A Christmas album – sort of! It has some good moments but marks a drop in quality compared to *Song of Seven* and *Animation*. (*Polydor*)

This page: Rick Wakeman from 1985 to 1987. This period saw Rick sign to President records, an indie label with rather more modest expectations than Charisma. Rock album *Silent Nights* is decent enough, although the live album from the promotional tour concentrated on classic 70s material. The period also spawned two pleasant 'new age' style albums, concentrating on the piano and *The Gospels*, a foray into the Christian market which charted in the UK, albeit at a lowly 94. (*President / Telstar / Coda*)

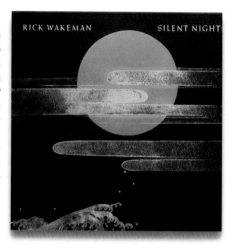

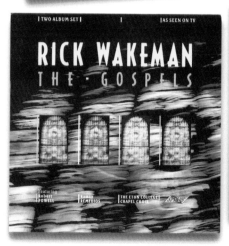

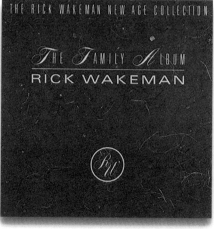

Left: *GTR*, the eponymous debut album from this some-might-argue contrived collaboration between Steve Howe and former Genesis guitarist Steve Hackett, plus some hired hands. The material is decent, but the 80s sonics make it almost unlistenable in places. (*Arista*)

Right: A healthy chart placing and a US hit single did mean that the project got noticed, as this cover of *Guitarist* in 1986 shows. (*David Watkinson Collection*)

WORLD'S MOST OFF THE WALL GUITARS

Guitar Player

PT.'86

FREE POSTER

STEVE HOWE
STEVE HACKETT

LARRY CARLTON
DARRYL JONES

US $2.95
Canada $3.95 UK £2.35

'86 READERS
POLL BALLOT

WIN A FREE
PAUL REED SMITH BASS

Left: ...and some money was spent on marketing, as this picture disk of the 'When The Heart Rules the Mind' single shows. It's shaped like a plectrum. Geddit? (*Arista*)

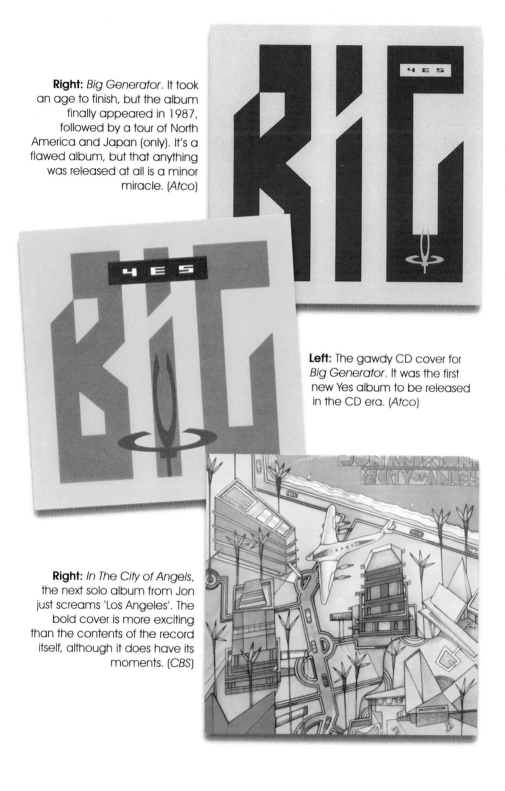

Right: *Big Generator*. It took an age to finish, but the album finally appeared in 1987, followed by a tour of North America and Japan (only). It's a flawed album, but that anything was released at all is a minor miracle. (*Atco*)

Left: The gawdy CD cover for *Big Generator*. It was the first new Yes album to be released in the CD era. (*Atco*)

Right: *In The City of Angels*, the next solo album from Jon just screams 'Los Angeles'. The bold cover is more exciting than the contents of the record itself, although it does have its moments. (*CBS*)

THE BIG TOUR JANUARY · FEBRUARY '88

JANUARY
			PA
SAT	16	....CREW ARRIVE	TALLAHASSEE, Fl
SUN	17	....BAND ARRIVE	TALLAHASSEE, FL
MON	18	....REHEARSAL	TALLAHASSEE, FL
TUE	19	....LEON COUNTY CIVIC CTR	TALLAHASSEE, FL
WED	20	....CIVIC CENTER	PENSACOLA, FL
THU	21	....DAY OFF	
FRI	22	....SUNDOME	TAMPA, FL
SAT	23	....SUNDOME	TAMPA, FL
SUN	24	....SPORTATORIUM	MIAMI, FL
MON	25	....DAY OFF	
TUE	26	....CIVIC CENTER	JACKSONVILLE, FL
WED	27	....DAY OFF	
THU	28	....THOMPSON BOILING ARENA	KNOXVILLE, TN
FRI	29	....OHIO CENTER	COLUMBUS, OH
SAT	30	....MARKET SQUARE. ARENA	INDIANAPOLIS, IN
SUN	31	....DAY OFF	

FEBRUARY
MON	1	....WINGS STADIUM	KALAMAZOO, MI
TUE	2	....TOLEDO SPORTS ARENA	TOLEDO, OH
WED	3	....DAY OFF	
THU	4	....HAMPTON COLISEUM	HAMPTON, VA
FRI	5	....NASSAU COLISEUM	UNIONDALE, NY
SAT	6	....BROOME COUNTY ARENA	BINGHAMTON, NY
SUN	7	....THE SPECTRUM	PHILADELPHIA, PA
MON	8	....HERSHEY PARK	HERSHEY, PA
TUE	9	....DAY OFF	
WED	10	....MUNICIPAL AUD. ARENA	NASHVILLE, TN
THU	11	....CHARLOTTE COLISEUM	CHARLOTTE, NC
FRI	12	....THE OMNI	ATLANTA, GA
SAT	13	....DEAN SMITH CENTER	CHAPEL HILL, NC
SUN	14	....DAY OFF	
MON	15	....DAY OFF	
TUE	16	....RICHFIELD COLISEUM	CLEVELAND, OH
WED	17	....RIVERFRONT COLISEUM	CINCINNATI, OH
THU	18	....DAY OFF	
FRI	19	....THE SUMMIT	HOUSTON, TX
SAT	20	....CAJUNDOME	LAFAYETTE
SUN	21	....REUNION ARENA	DALLAS, TX
MON	22	....FRANK ERWIN CENTER	AUSTIN, TX

Big Generator Tour *SET LIST*

Almost Like Love (*) (1)
Rhythm of Love
Final Eyes (*)
I'm Running (*)
Hold On
Heart Of The Sunrise
Big Generator
Changes
Shoot High Aim Low
Holy Lamb (2)
Solly's Beard
Make It Easy intro/Owner Of A Lonely Heart
Yours Is No Disgrace
Excerpt from Ritual (*)/Amazing Grace (3)
And You And I
Starship Trooper: Wurm
Love Will Find A Way (4)
I've Seen All Good People
Roundabout (5)
Donguri Koro Koro (6)

Notes
1. Only played in first part of the tour. It was the opening song.
2. Early on, "Holy Lamb" was merged with "Wurm".
3. Occasionally, Jon would sing "Amazing Grace" while Chris played. Chris also (at least once) threw in a few licks from "On The Silent Wings Of Freedom".
4. Early on, "Love Will Find a Way" was played acoustically.
5. In Japan, Trevor had hurt his hand. They didn't play "Roundabout" then, but Jon did a solo performance of "Soon" as an encore.
6. Donguri Koro Koro (means "Acorn Rolling Rolling") was performed in Japan only.

Sources
Springfield 11/19/87
Philadelphia, PA 11/30/87
Charlotte, VA 1987
Hollywood, FL 1/29/88
Tokyo, Japan 1988
Yokohama, Japan 1988

• Front cover feature of *Guitar World plus* large article.

Personnel
Jon Anderson
Tony Kaye
Trevor Rabin
Chris Squire
Alan White

JANUARY 1988
£1.40

MUSIC *technology*

YES
Walk the Dinosaur

ON TEST
Microdeal Super Conductor
Simmons Silicon Mallet
E-mu SP1200 Sampler
Korg DSM1 Sampler
Steinberg Time-Lock
Digidesign Q-Sheet
XRI Synchroniser
Apple Hypercard

THE CHRISTIANS
"Challenging stereotypes"

ARP ODYSSEY
The forgotten synth

SCORING A VIDEO
Putting music to pictures

Above: A British Yes fan – without the opportunity to see the *Big Generator* tour – could dream. This little collage acts as a tribute to that tour – painstakingly compiling the dates and set list from various sources. (*David Watkinson Collection*)

Left: Even in 1988, there was still interest from the technical magazines. Here, Rabin and Kaye appear on the cover of the January 1988 issue of *Music Technology*. (*David Watkinson Collection*)

Right: Rick Wakeman in 1988 and 1989. This is a varied bunch of albums. The much scaled-down *Time Machine* project was financed by Polydor, but released on President, with guest vocalists Roy Wood and John Parr. The 'new age' albums continued, although *Zodiaque* is actually rather interesting, based around the percussion of Tony Fernandez. (*President / Ambient*)

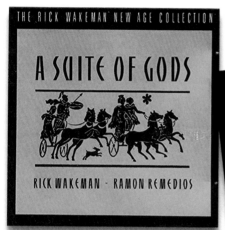

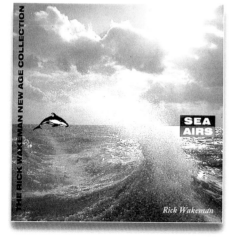

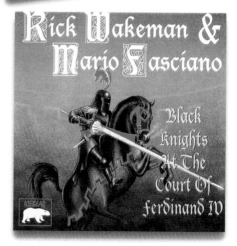

Left: *Anderson, Bruford, Wakeman, Howe.* Was it Yes? Was it a Jon Anderson solo project? Was it even a band? The album is patchy but excellent in places, containing some music that – arguably – would never have appeared on a Yes album. (*Arista / Esoteric*)

Below: Brian Lane chats to Bill Bruford and an unnamed staff member circa 1989. Lane was the main catalyst behind the formation of Asia, GTR and Anderson, Bruford, Wakeman, Howe.

Left: The talented sidemen behind the 1989 ABWH tour – Tony Levin, Julian Colebeck and Milton MacDonald – from the tour programme. (*David Watkinson Collection*)

Right: Jon during the ABWH concert at Wembley in 1989. (*David Watkinson Collection*)

Left: Rick chats to the audience at the same show. The solo sets at the start of the concert gave the shows a unique ambience. (*David Watkinson Collection*)

Right: Bruford and Levin on stage on 1989. The shot gives an excellent view of Bruford's largely electronic kit. (*David Watkinson Collection*)

Left: Another tour, another bold 1980s stage set, with design by Roger Dean.

Right: Steve Howe playing the excellent 'Birthright' during the 1989 ABWH US tour.

Left: Bill Bruford behind the (electric) kit in 1989.

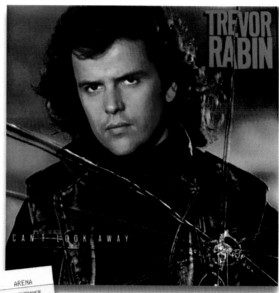

Right: *Can't Look Away*. Trevor Rabin's 1989 solo album co-produced by the legendary Bob Ezrin. (*Electra*)

Left: Seeing ABWH in October 1989 would cost you £14.50 – it was an expensive ticket for the time and a tripling of the cost of seeing Yes in 1980. (*David Watkinson Collection*)

Right: Released in 1991, Howe's excellent instrumental rock album *Turbulence* was mainly recorded in 1988 and 1989, after GTR but before ABWH. A couple of riffs were to turn up on *Union*. (*Relativity*)

This page: In that pre-internet age, fanzines were a vital source of information for Yes fans. These were often international collaborations. Jon Dee's *Yes Music* was the one with the highest production values, but *Relayer*, produced by Tanya Coad in Canada and Sue Smith in the USA, was also a vital source of information, as was *Close to the Yes*, a collaboration between Mario Gronevald in the Netherlands and Carol Pynn in the UK. (*David Watkinson Collection*)

yes music

4 & 5

WORLD EXCLUSIVE

CHRIS & CO.
- IN THE
STUDIO !

ASIA &
ANDERSON
- U.S.
TOUR
REVIEWS

Issue #5

Relayer

CLOSE TO YES

DECEMBER '87 / JANUARI '88

nigel

YES LIVE IN OMAHA !

1988 – Anderson Regains Control

Jon Anderson – *In The City of Angels*

Personnel:

Jon Anderson: vocals, harp, drums, percussion

Steve Lukather: guitar (track 10)

Steve Porcaro: keyboard programming (track 10)

Jeff Porcaro: drums (track 2, 4 & 10)

Mike Porcaro: bass (tracks 2 & 4)

David Paich: keyboards, orchestration (tracks 2, 4, 6 & 10)

Joseph Williams: backing vocals (track 10)

Larry Williams: keyboards, programming (tracks 1, 3, 5 & 9)

John Robinson: drums (tracks 1, 3, 7-9)

Paul Jackson Jr.: guitar (tracks 1 & 5)

Jimmy Haslip: bass (track 1, 5, 7 & 8)

Lenny Castro: percussion (tracks 1, 3, 5 & 7)

Dann Huff: guitar (tracks 2, 4 & 8)

Michael Landau: guitar (tracks 2, 4, 7-9 & 11)

Marc Russo: saxophone (track 4)

Paulinho Da Costa: percussion (tracks 4 & 8)

Gordon Peeke: drum programming (track 7)

Don Freeman: keyboards (tracks 7 & 8)

Jerry Hey: trumpet (track 7)

Gary Grant: trumpet (track 7)

Bill Reichenbach Jr.: sax, trombone (tracks 7 & 9)

Kim Hutchcroft: sax (track 7)

Rhett Lawrence: keyboards, programming (Tracks 9 & 11)

The Cathedral Choir: backing vocals (track 11)

Recorded at Ocean Way Studio, Hollywood

Produced by Stuart Levine

Released May 7 1988

Chart placing: UK: Did not chart USA: Did not chart.

1. Hold on to Love (Anderson, Lamont Dozier) 2. If It Wasn't for Love (Oneness Family) (Anderson) 3. Sundancing (For the Hopi/Navajo Energy) (Anderson) 4. Is It Me (Anderson, Rhett Lawrence) 5. In a Lifetime (Anderson, Dozier) 6. For You (Anderson, David Paich) 7. New Civilization (Anderson, Don Freeman, Gordon Peeke) 8. It's on Fire (Anderson, Freeman) 9. Betcha (Anderson, Lawrence) 10. Top of the World (The Glass Bead Game) 11. Hurry Home (Song from The Pleiades) (Anderson)

If the process of recording *Big Generator* had not been the easiest, then the tour that began in November 1987 and continued – with some breaks – until the middle of April 1988 seemed harmonious enough. Indeed, the band were part of the Atlantic Records 40ᵗʰ Anniversary party at their spiritual home of Madison Square Gardens on 14 April. It's significant, however, that the 70-date tour only left North America briefly to go to Japan for eight concerts just prior to the Atlantic records show. There was no attempt to play Europe.

As we've already seen with the many and various collaborative projects that Anderson was involved in away from the band during the tortuous recording process for *Big Generator,* the vocalist was distinctly underused during the two-year period. While he's hardly missing from the writing credits, it's clear that his position in the band had been very different since he rejoined in 1983. This was bound to come to a head, and it did so at the end of the tour. His role as band 'leader' had been usurped by Rabin and Squire – he was now just the singer and his input, while not ignored, was clearly much reduced.

It seems that the straw that broke the camels back as far as Anderson was concerned, as he told *Raw* magazine, was the refusal of the band to rehearse 'Close to the Edge', instead sticking to tried and trusted material, mainly from the past two albums. It's hardly surprising that they didn't – Kaye and Rabin had never played it, and it would have felt like a major left-field step to play such a lengthy piece in the current circumstances. However, it shows the gulf that had opened up between Anderson and his four bandmates in terms of their perception of what Yes should be.

Anderson's departure coincided with the end of the tour and the release of his next solo album, *In the City of Angels,* in May 1988. Via his then-management team at Lookout Management, he had signed a solo deal with the prestigious CBS records. This must have seemed like a good deal for CBS at the time. Here, after all, was the vocalist with the band that had had a number one smash with 'Owner Of A Lonely Heart', and it's *all* about the singer, right?

Conceived and recorded in 1987 and completed in 1988, the album was released in May 1988, at which point Anderson announced his departure from Yes with little fuss or fanfare. The album was coordinated and produced by California-based producer Stewart Levine. Levin's CV is astonishing, having produced albums – and indeed hits – for artists like Sly Stone, The Crusaders and Boz Scaggs. It's no coincidence that most of his work had been within the pop/soul genre, so would Anderson's new project follow the formula? In one word – yes.

The title *In the City Of Angels* says it all, really. This is an album directly influenced by Los Angeles, the city in which it was recorded. It has a smooth, synth-dominated vibe, with Anderson composing with the cream of West Coast songwriting talent, including Motown legend Lamont Dozier and 'safe pair of hands' songwriter/producer Rhett Lawrence. Not that Anderson's natural upbeat exuberance is entirely repressed, of course. No vocalist sounds like him, for a start, and the songs are all tuneful at worst – a pleasant listen in an undemanding way. There are even presages of what was to come the following year, particularly in the fanfare-style synths of 'Sundancing', which suggests the similar work on *Anderson, Bruford, Wakeman, Howe.*

Broadly, the album was recorded by two 'teams' of session players, with most of the parts played by well-connected musicians like drummer John Robinson, keyboardist Larry Williams, bassist Jimmy Haslip and legendary session guitarist Michael Landau. These pieces are all pleasant enough in a homogenous 1980s way. The Dozier co-writes 'In A Lifetime' and the lead single 'Hold On To Love' both exude class (and look out for Chris Squire in the video for the latter), even if neither became the hits they probably deserved to be. Lyrically, Anderson revels in his natural impulse towards sentimentality – here given full rein – as well as his interest in Native American history, culture and spirituality.

However, many Yes fans seem to prefer the pieces that were co-written and co-produced by David Paich. Paich, of course, is best known for his work with Toto, but his CV includes work with Boz Scaggs and Michael Jackson, and he contributes several co-writes to the album, including the charming 'For You' and the mini-prog epic (yes, the album does have one) 'Top Of The World (The Glass bead Game)'. This latter track is essentially by Anderson and an uncredited Toto, featuring as it does the only appearance on the album from the band's guitarist Steve Lukather and vocalist Joseph Williams, while Paich also gets to sing a little and the Porcaro brothers Mike and Jeff provide the rhythm section. It's a terrific piece. As we've already seen, Anderson returned the favour with a guest appearance on Toto's wonderful single 'Stop Loving You' from their album *The Seventh One*, recorded at the same time as *The City Of Angels*.

Overall, while *In The City Of Angels* may feel a little bland and homogenized to some, it was a worthy attempt to re-brand Anderson as a pop vocalist. It might have come off. But it didn't, and the album – while well marketed, once again – sank without trace both in the USA and the UK. Aged 44, his pop career was over almost before it had begun. Again. What next for the vocalist?

Anderson, Bruford, Wakeman, Howe

Personnel:
Jon Anderson: Vocals
Steve Howe: Guitars
Rick Wakeman: Keyboards
Bill Bruford: Electronic and Acoustic Drums
Tony Levin: Bass, Stick, Vocals
Matt Clifford: Keyboards, Programming, Orchestration, Vocals
Milton McDonald: Rhythm Guitar
Backing vocals: The Oxford Circus Singers – Deborah Anderson, Tessa Niles, Carol Kenyon, Francis Dunnery. JMC Singers – Jon Anderson, Matt Clifford, Chris Kimsey. Emerald Community Singers, Monserrat.
Produced by Chris Kimsey and Jon Anderson at Air Studios, Monserrat and Air Studios, London. Pre-production recording at Studio La Frette, Paris.
Released: 20 June 1989
All compositions by Anderson, Wakeman, Bruford, Howe. Additional writing credits shown under tracklisting
Highest chart places: UK: 14, USA: 30
1. Themes i. Sound ii. Second Attention iii. Soul Warrior 2. Fist of Fire 3. Brother of Mine i. The Big Dream ii. Nothing Can Come Between Us iii. Long Lost Brother of Mine (Geoff Downes) 4. Birthright   (Max Bacon) 5. The Meeting 6. Quartet i. I Wanna Learn ii. She Gives Me Love (Ben Dowling) iii. Who Was the First iv. I'm Alive 7. Teakbois 8. Order of the Universe i. Order Theme ii. Rock Gives Courage (Rhett Lawrence) iii. It's So Hard to Grow iv. The Universe 9. Let's Pretend (Vangelis)

The 'next' turned out to be an entirely different project entirely and the instigator seems to have been Anderson's wife, Jennifer. Like Squire's wife Nikki seems to have been, Jennifer had always been an opinionated and high-profile 'wag' in the Yes fold, and here she was no different. There's no doubting the wisdom in her suggestion, though. As Anderson told Sid Smith on the sleeve notes to the Esoteric reissue in 2014: 'She wanted me to do an album that was more like classic Yes, because she felt that people were missing that sound.' Yes indeed.

Whereas *Drama* has been conceived by Chris Squire as a return to the spirit of *The Yes Album*, Jon moved one album further along and hatched a plan to record a project with the *Fragile / Close to the Edge* line up of the band – himself, Steve Howe, Rick Wakeman, Chris Squire and Bill Bruford. Was this a solo project? Was it to be Yes? It was never completely clear to anyone, probably not even to Anderson, at the time, although when Brian Lane was again brought in to oversee the project from a management perspective, some members – particularly the always-canny Bruford – smelled a rat. True to form, Anderson was chancing his arm. Howe, Wakeman and Bruford all agreed to take part, with Bruford at least under the impression that he would be playing on a Jon Anderson solo record. He visited each musician in turn to gather material and ideas. Howe provided a small treasure trove of material, while Anderson himself, always working on new music as he was, had a mixture of new and old material, including one piece he had written with Rhett Lawrence ('Rock Gives Courage') during the *In The City Of Angels* writing sessions. Howe's pieces included two songs originally conceived during writing sessions with Geoff Downes and Max Bacon for Asia and GTR in 'Birthright' and 'Long Lost Brother of Mine'. With Lane's help, a recording contract with Arista was signed.

Initially, Anderson began to accumulate all the material that had come in from each of musicians. Howe and Bruford both lived within spitting distance of London; Howe in Hampstead Garden Suburb and Bruford in Surrey. He also spent a couple of days with Wakeman, who at that point lived on the Isle of Man. Then he moved to Studio La Frette Studio in Paris to develop the pieces with keyboard player Matt Clifford and Milton McDonald on guitar, plus programmer Jon Hamer and Clem Clempson on guitar and an uncredited drummer. It was here that he produced demos for about 80% of the album. The plan was then that he would get the three musicians to record their own parts, replacing much of the demo material with their own personal magic. Bruford confirms this in his autobiography:

So now Jon was bringing in the A-team to sprinkle fairy dust on the demo parts to make it a bit more personal. The invitation to record what I still thought of as at that time as being a Jon Anderson solo album in Monsarrat, was the deal clincher.

The chosen location for this recording was Air Studios, Montserrat. Hardly a cheap location, but a relaxed, informal one. For Bruford, a working holiday in the Caribbean was the icing on the cake. Indeed, the brief footage on the *Big Dream* DVD shows the drummer to be in rare, jocular form, clearly enjoying his surroundings, as is Wakeman.

There were only two flies in the ointment. One was that Jon was holding out for Chris Squire to join the project on bass. This may have been a naïve view. Squire was still holding the 'official' Yes reigns with Rabin, Kaye and White on the West coast of the USA. His participation was surely a long shot. Furthermore, Bruford suggested that he would rather not work with Squire, instead suggesting his King Crimson bandmate Tony Levin. The American had – and still enjoys – a reputation as a musician of professionalism and talent. Furthermore, he is easy to get along with. When Anderson realised that Levin would arrive well-prepared, he was convinced. Levin, too, came to the Caribbean.

The other was Steve Howe. Howe flatly refused to go to Montserrat. The guitarist – always one to demand control of his recording environment – elected to record his parts at Air Studios in London, away from Anderson, Wakeman and Bruford. Anderson was not best pleased, as 'the plan was the plan' and his idea was that the musicians would bond and so create their best work on the island, perhaps reproducing those heady days creating *Fragile* in London in 1971. But that's not really Howe's way. The guitarist's plan was – reluctantly – accepted. Although he planned to produce, Arista did not quite trust Anderson to co-ordinate the project on his own, so appointed the experienced knob-twiddler Chris Kimsey. Best known for his work with The Rolling Stones, Kimsey had also just worked with Marillion on their two hit albums *Misplaced Childhood* and *Clutching At Straws*. He was used to working with bands that contained big personalities and was an excellent choice in the circumstances. Anderson was not happy about having Kimsey imposed on him, but one suspects that he wasn't given any option.

But why did Howe, Wakeman and Bruford become involved in the project? It's not hard to see why Wakeman and Howe did. Both musicians were at something of an impasse. For Howe, 1988 was a busy year but a 'bity' one. With GTR – disappointingly – at an end, he had no 'band' project, and much of the year was taken up with guest appearances. He had also been working off and on, on his solo album *Turbulence*, which also featured Bill Bruford. Howe described the situation in his autobiography:

I invited John to our house on the edge of Hampstead Garden Suburb. We had a few laughs as if nothing too insurmountable had happened and he left with the cassette [of songs]. This was to be the start of some really convoluted recording experiences. I can say it was simply a mindboggling time that began with the recording of the ABWH album.

John had had enough for a while, at least at the Los Angeles Yes set up. Chris, whom John clearly loved, have been getting harder to work with. The members of each new incarnation of Yes needed to stand on solid ground as they completely relied on each other. This quality is an essential key that can unlock any bands progress. Reliability and trust are the glue that buy musicians together to create great performances. Lack of it has played havoc throughout my career.

Wakeman was still not having the best of things. The last couple of years had been unkind with several disappointing projects behind him, including the undercooked *Time Machine* album (discussed shortly), which had begun backed by Polydor as a full-scale album with orchestra and choir, but had petered out into another disappointing rock album, released on an indie label. His *Gospels* project – although it had involved a concert at the Royal Albert Hall in May 1987 – had also failed to set the world alight. He was perhaps beginning to feel that his solo career as a chart musician might be behind him for the time being and he wasn't even 40.

Bruford was also repositioning himself as a jazz musician – albeit one that used the best that the new electronic percussion could offer. This came with many benefits, including creative freedom, but it also came with a drop in stature and audiences. The rest of his career was to take in jazz with other, sometimes more-rock orientated projects, and, later, a move back to acoustic drums and after retirement from playing, teaching in Guildford. Your author spent a happy couple of hours with Bill at a café in Guildford in 2009 discussing his career. And Bill, always the gentleman, paid for the coffee. But for the next couple of years, he was back on the Yes treadmill, in one way or another.

Finally, the album was recorded. Howe, as was his habit and left to his own devices over a period of two weeks, had layered guitars all over the record. As a result, he was unimpressed with the final mix by Steve Thompson and Michael Barbiero, saying:

Sadly, instead of staying as a homespun British sounding album, *Anderson Bruford, Wakeman Howe* was farmed out to a mixing team, who were very popular at the time, but who appeared to have no idea about the internal instrument balance that we developed over the years. A crucial part of Yes.

135

He may have a point, in that Thompson and Barbiero were known as a 'team' at the time, with their own brand of mixing 'fairy dust', producing mixes that were label-friendly, but which displeased Howe:

> The style of mixing wasn't to my liking. Parts and textures could have been balanced more effectively. 'Vultures in the City' isn't on the album. It became the B-side of the single 'Brother of Mine'. But in its extended form, it was quite something. Unfortunately, the editing left it lacking.

So, what are we to make of *Anderson, Bruford, Wakeman, Howe?* It seems to sit slightly uncomfortably alongside – but arguably not within – the Yes canon. Anderson's complete control produced some music that might never have appeared on a Yes album, although there is much to suggest a progressive direction that Yes might have taken in the 1980s had they not settled on the enhanced AOR of the *Big Generator* era. The overall sound is progressive in many places, but modern too, especially via the interesting – but somewhat dated, now – textures provided by Bruford's electronic drums.

If there's an overall problem, it stems from the way that the album was constructed prior to the trip to Montserrat in Paris. The band of 1971 and 1972, which was nominally the template for this album, would have laboured hard over transitions and the intricacies of arrangement. However, by the time the band convened in the Caribbean, the vast majority of these decisions had already been taken several weeks before when the demos were created, over which the final picture was to be painted. As a result, the longer tracks – especially 'Brother Of Mine' and 'The Order Of The Universe' – have one-dimensional arrangements that feel like what they are, which is short pieces bumped together to make longer ones. As a result, the album feels like something of a hybrid; part Jon Anderson solo album, part group recording. So, for some, the album is a return to the progressive group dynamic of the 1970s, while for others, it's a patchy mish-mash of ideas.

Despite this, the location of the recording and the relaxed manner in which the final keyboard and percussion parts were created should not be understated, Wakeman noted on the sleeve notes for the Esoteric reissue:

> Being there also allowed for spontaneity as the studio was on permanent call. Which meant that if you felt like recording at any time you could. John and I wrote 'The Meeting' at about two in the morning. The timing

was perfect. Interestingly enough, Bill was very responsible in many ways for what I did with that album and created such amazingly beautiful and clever percussion timings and sounds that I used to latch onto these a lot. That helped create what I played. Similarly with Tony Levin's bass work. You can't help but be inspired by great musicians.

Released at a time when CD was just starting to challenge the sales figures of vinyl, the band's self-titled album is a long record for those buying it on the traditional plastic, as I did. Too long, in fact. As a sequence of pieces of music, it doesn't really hang together. The band could quite easily have dropped the charming but lightweight 'Quartet' and the Caribbean-influenced cheese-fest that is 'Teakbois', both of which see Anderson convincing Wakeman and Howe to play parts that might have seemed alien to them in any other project, including Yes. That said, the pretend-trumpet in 'Quartet' is a pleasant, Beatle-esque diversion and the opening section of the same song is clearly a repurposed Howe solo piece, with the guitarist multi-tracking delightfully. As a complete piece, though, it's wafer-thin. 'Teakbois', on the other hand, is the least Yes-like track this side of 'Man in The Moon' (from *Open Your Eyes*). It's an Anderson solo piece, pure and simple, and the rest of the band are his support players. As mentioned by Howe, another track, 'Vultures In The City', was recorded for the album. It's good, a slow-burning, atmospheric piece – particularly in its long version – written largely by Howe. However, arguably it's 'more of the same' and given that vinyl was still dominant, if something had to give, it was probably the right decision to drop it. As I've said, the album is too long anyway.

However, there's better news. Levin sounds right at home, accompanying Bruford's big, booming electronic drums with his trademark languid, finger-style bass lines. It's arguably better for this music than anything that Squire might have produced. Indeed, it's safe to say that while *Fragile* might have been the template, there's nothing here that sounds remotely like that classic album, so Squire really isn't missed. But this album is unique as that famous record was. Wakeman survives some typically odd synth patches to deliver some fine playing, including some lovely piano and Howe's contributions are excellent throughout, with more distorted tones than we are used to thirty years later. He also benefits from the restraint given to his parts by the out-of-house mixing team, who do an excellent job, to these ears at least.

NO!

ANDERSON BRUFORD WAKEMAN HOWE: hovering between disappointing, absolutely dreadful and complete crap

ANDERSON BRUFORD WAKEMAN HOWE
'Anderson Bruford Wakeman Howe'
(Arista 209970)

K

THE MUCH-MUTTERED opinion that the recent 'reformation' (almost) of this classic Yes line-up was prompted by other than burning musical ambitions/desires may appear in some quarters to be nothing more than a case of only-to-be-expected journalistic backbiting.

The resultant personnel-titled album, however, is nothing if not a gallon or two of highly inflammable material chucked on to these smouldering embers of doubt.

On listening to this album you'd be hard pushed to detect that there were four-fifths of the creative quintet that produced such musical milestones as 'Tales From Topographic Oceans', 'Close To The Edge' and 'Fragile' playing on the thing.

The only glaring clue to past glories is Jon Anderson's thin, fragile, helium-balloon vocals and lyrical input, the latter a stream of his embarrassingly ridiculous, rambling lines that would suggest that author is a fully qualified space cadet with a couple of cards short of the full deck.

What is particularly ironic is that the drumming of Bill Bruford – the only member who, prior to this reformation, has produced some staggeringly accomplished and innovative work on a series of albums with his own band, and latterly on a trio of exquisite albums with the muscular King Crimson – is either under-used or non-existent.

With his potentially face-saving contribution strangled, the instrumental baton is handed in turn to guitarist Steve Howe and keyboardsman Rick Wakeman, both of whom appear to have lost the creative spark and whose stilted accompaniments and vacuous solos produce little of what might have been hoped for and certainly leave a lot to be desired.

That the collective instrumental punch is reduced to a slap on the wrist isn't at all surprising considering the vehicles of expression that they've lumbered themselves with.

At best uninspired, at worst depressingly dull and trite, the songs often sound fragmented and lacking in direction, with more than a couple giving the impression that they might easily have been chucked together in the time it took for the kettle to boil and recording completed before the tea had gone cold.

Side One is disappointing to say the least, Side Two is absolutely dreadful and, even objectively, 'Anderson Wakeman Bruford Howe' offers extremely little.

Subjectively, I'd have to say that, with due respect to their past, it's complete crap.

PAUL HENDERSON

YESTERDAYS?

BAND: **ANDERSON BRUFORD WAKEMAN HOWE**
VENUE: **WEMBLEY ARENA**
DATE: **29/10/89**

What's in a name? Legally, Anderson Bruford Wakeman Howe can't call themselves 'Yes'. Musically, you can't really call them anything else! Therefore, tonight's show had been billed as 'An Evening Of Yes Music'.

It was the second of two sold out shows at Wembley Arena (Anderson still referred to the venue as the 'Empire Pool') and a capacity audience (ranging in age from 5 to 50) eagerly awaited the return of a '70s phenomenon.

The familiar strains of The Firebird Suite heralded the start of the show as a solo spotlight picked out vocalist Jon Anderson amidst the crowd singing Time And A Word as he gracefully moved his way onto the stage before breaking into excerpts from 'Owner Of A Lonely Heart' and 'Teakbois'. Howe, Wakeman and Bruford followed suit to rapturous applause as they played their various intro pieces. Two decades on, Anderson's choirboy singing, Howe's old acoustic showcase, and the rowdiest blasts from Bruford and Wakeman have ceased to be over self-indulgent displays for the worshipful masses. Instead, they were warm and welcoming!

Showcasing their 'Yes Music' the band came across as powerful and majestic as they ever were. Long Distance Runaround, And You And I and the spontaneous I've Seen All Good People displayed excesses of energy. Complete with a gigantic spider backdrop (courtesy of the Dean brothers) this could well have been seen as 'classic' Anderson Bruford Wake ... er Yes! Submerged in billows of dry ice Anderson's gentle voice transcended into magic as he broke into Soon The Light. He told the crowd that they were wonderful, the band's energy was their energy, a reflection, a circle, a kind of cosmic magic. Of course, everyone seemed pleased to go along with that!

New album cuts such as 'Birthright', Themes and The Meeting fitted in perfectly with the older material, while Brother Of Mine and 'Order Of The Universe' stood out as classics in their own right, showing that creative versatility still abounds. Arguably, Yes Music (a concept in itself, whoever may contribute to it) has thrown up two of the 80s most exciting songs, namely 'Owner Of A Lonely Heart' on the one hand (or the other!) and 'Brother Of Mine'. The latter being a masterpiece of modern music!

Bassist Tony Levin, with his finger extensions, augmented the band admirably although the Squire 'magic' was most noticeably missing! Nothing would have pleased me more than to see Chris Squire up there alongside Mrs Anderson, Wakeman, Bruford and Howe! The presence of the fish' would have made the combination almost perfect!

Rick Wakeman, behind a mountain of keyboards, launched the combo into 'Close To The Edge' which proved to be the religious highlight of the show. As the stage set began to take on almost 'alter-like shape the priests' of rock threw everything they had into their music, Howe and Wakeman being definitive exponents of their art forms.

Heart Of The Sunrise saw guitarist Steve Howe in his 'element' as he jumped around the stage brandishing his Gibson. Bill Bruford's flamboyant drumming introduced time signatures that have yet to be discovered! Showmen all!

The Wembley crowd cried out the band's name (you know the other one) and they came back to encore with 'Roundabout' and 'Starship Trooper' as the lighting rig pinged down in rays of crystal clear light over the well satisfied 'congregation'. Ecstasy wasn't the word for it!

Tonight's show was a musical education if nothing else. A trip down memory lane perhaps? Anderson Bruford Wakeman Howe put their emphasis on the music as opposed to the elaborate 'Big' stage show of 90125 Yes (the other lot).

I'm sure as we race towards the year 2000 that Yes Music will blossom and flower into something greater. But for the moment it is as important in this computerised, computerised, saturised and businesswised world as it was 'eons' ago! The name may change but the music will still stir the memories. Anderson's voice will be as unmistakable in the '90s as it was in the previous two decades. Be it 1969, 1979 or even 1989 there is still life in the old dog yet.

YES INDEED!

REVIEWER: **MARK CRAMPTON**
LIVE SHOTS: **Courtesy of PICTORIAL PRESS**

Above: Reviews for the ABWH album were mixed. Here's a rather damning one from *Kerrang*. (*David Watkinson Collection*)

Left: The live shows were better received, however, as shown by the review by Mark Crampton in *Riff Raff* magazine. (*David Watkinson Collection*)

The album has a strong start in 'Themes', although Howe shows some disdain for it in his autobiography, since he had no part in its creation. However, it's s strong opening and there are certainly elements of Yesness about it, with the individual musicians introduced one by one, until Howe arrives during the 'Second Attention' section. 'Fist Of Fire' is an album highlight. It's short and rhythmic; a hard-edged piece, most notable for some thrilling playing from Wakeman – either Minimoog or a really good approximation – ably supported by Howe. Incidentally, a different mix can be found on the *In a Word* compilation, which has some of the other parts that Howe recorded for the track restored. Honestly, that version is more cluttered. I may be biased as a Wakeman fanboy, but it's Rick's playing that deserves the limelight here.

'Brother Of Mine' is the first of the 'showcase' tracks, with a single edit and a glossy video used to promote the album. It's a powerful, well-constructed piece, built from material written by Anderson and a 'chorus' written by Howe with Geoff Downes. If the album has a real classic, it's probably 'Birthright', which is based on material written by Howe with GTR vocalist Max Bacon. Bacon presumably provided lyrics – there are words here which don't sound like the sort that Anderson would write. But it gives Howe the opportunity to build a piece around his classical guitar, and then add layers of electric guitar as the track builds. Bruford's percussion moves away from the bombast of previous pieces to provide something a lot more textural. If it's a signal of a direction this band might have taken, it's a strong one – and a damn shame that it wasn't pursued.

There's very little written by Anderson and Wakeman as a team on record prior to their somewhat undercooked 2011 album as a duo, *The Living Tree*. It's impossible to take the pieces they wrote together that later appeared as *The Paris Sessions* at face value, since they were incomplete and recorded by a splintering band, so 'The Meeting' is another example of 'what might have been' in a band context. It's simple, charming and Wakeman's piano is delightful. Indeed, this was the only song to have a life beyond the Anderson, Bruford, Wakeman, Howe project, as the two played it during Yes' 2004 world tour.

As already mentioned, 'side two' begins relatively weakly with the (arguably) superfluous 'Quartet' and the quirky-at-best 'Teakbois' before coming to life with the second showpiece of the album, 'The Order of The Universe'. Again, this suggests a direction that the band might have taken, opening with a very strong synth 'theme', choral voices and some of the hardest rock the musicians have ever played. It's impressive stuff, and the song was equally impressive live. Again, despite its length, the music is very different to what Yes might have created, but it works. The album ends on another lovely ballad, 'Let's Pretend', written by Anderson with Vangelis, which showcases Howe's multitracked guitars.

Anderson, Wakeman and Bruford confessed themselves happy with the final product and parted as friends, having agreed to tour the album. Howe was furious – without justification, it could be argued – about the way his guitar parts had been utilised but was finally persuaded to join the group on the tour. They had become a band!

Rick Wakeman – *Time Machine*

Personnel:
Rick Wakeman: keyboards, composition. production
David Paton: bass
Tony Fernandez: drums, percussion
Ashley Holt: vocals (4 & 8)
John Knightsbridge: guitar (4 & 9)
John Parr: vocals (2 & 9)
Roy Wood: vocals (1)
Tracy Ackerman: vocals (3, 5 & 6)
Recorded June to October 1987, at Studio House, Wraysbury, Berkshire
Released 1988
Tracklisting: 1. Custer's Last Stand 2. Ocean City 3. Angel of Time 4. Slaveman 5. Ice 6. Open Up Your Eyes 7. Elizabethan Rock 8. Make Me A Woman 9. Rock Age

Rick Wakeman – *Suite of The Gods*

Personnel:
Rick Wakeman: keyboards, composition. production
Tony Fernandez: percussion
Ramon Remedios: tenor
Released: 1988
Tracklisting: 1. Dawn of Time 2. The Oracle 3. Pandora's Box 4. Chariot of the Sun 5. The Flood 6. The Voyage of Ulysses 7. Hercules

Tony Fernandez and Rick Wakeman – *Zodiaque*

Personnel:
Rick Wakeman: keyboards, composition. production
Tony Fernandez: percussion, composition

Released: 1988

Tracklisting: 1. Sagittarius 2. Capricorn 3. Gemini 4. Cancer 5. Pisces 6. Aquarius 7. Aries 8. Libra 9. Leo 10. Virgo 11. Taurus 12. Scorpio

Rick had spent a great deal of time in the mid-1980s trying to get another major project off the ground, based around *The Time Machine* by H.G Wells. Initially, to be funded by Polydor, initial sessions did not go well, and the Gospels project became Rick's priority at the time. The album was finally finished in 1987 in a much-scaled down form – there was no orchestra or choir, although guest appearances from pop legend Roy Wood and hit vocalist John Parr did add a little star power. The album was finally sold by Polydor to President records, who released it in July 1988. Rick has made a few – sometimes contradictory – things about it over the years, saying in his autobiography, '...I had lost interest in it the time it hit the shops'. However, on *rwcc.com* he is now somewhat more positive:

I think some of the songwriting on this album is some of the best I have ever written. 'Ocean City' and 'Custer's Last Stand' are two of my favourites and 'Ice', is for me the best overall song I have ever written. Worth having in my book!

He has a point, although if ever an album in the Wakey back catalogue has aged badly, it's this one. It's awash with 80s-sounding reverb, electronic drums and keyboard patches. Rick is right in that the songwriting is pretty decent, and there are some terrific moments. An ascending chord sequence on 'Ocean City' sounds made for Yes. Lesser-known vocalist Tracey Ackerman does her best attempt at creating a choir (without huge successs). But there are also some cringe-inducing moments – Ashley Holt screeching his way through 'Slaveman' and the blues ballad 'Make Me A Woman' being two of them, while twee instrumental 'Elizabethan Rock' has not stood the test of time especially well. 'Ice' – as Rick says – is a lost classic, and David Paton's bass playing is also a high point throughout. A supporter of Rick's solo work up to this point, I jumped ship around this time, but I'm glad I caught up with this album eventually, despite its obvious flaws.

Rick spoke about a very different album – *Suite of The Gods* – on *rwcc.com:*

This, for me, is a little masterpiece. It was recorded in the mid-eighties and used one of the first computer recording packages that was about as stable as Iraq. The software was very primitive and crashed at regular intervals. All the sounds were keyboard created with the exception of the percussion, which again, although played by Tony Fernandez, was in fact electronic. The vocals were some of the best ever recorded by Ramon Remedios and all in all, I was very proud of this album and only wish it could have been performed live.

Rick sums up the album nicely, the cover art making it very clear that it's a new age product. It is quite restful, but it's clear that Rick's ambitions for it were much less 'niche' than that. The album is lovely, in an undemanding way, and whether you enjoy it will depend on whether you like classical tenor singing and Rick's attempts to approximate an orchestra using 1980s technology.

Rick is often at his best when interpreting the music of other artists, and the *Zodiaque* album takes as its cues from percussion patterns – many of them electronic – created by Tony Fernandez. Hats off to the talented and long-serving percussionist for his contributions to this album and of Rick's new age efforts, this turns out to be one of the best. There is a track for each sign of the Zodiac (thus the title) and despite the 1980s keyboard textures, this is one of the more listenable albums from the era, and unlike anything else in his catalogue.

1989 – The New 'Yes' Triumphant

With the album complete and a Roger Dean cover secured, the eponymous *Anderson, Bruford, Wakeman, Howe* album was released in June 1989 to a decent reception and better sales – 700 000, eventually – than anyone might have expected (mind you, I've bought it three times). This was some way south of the figure achieved by *Big Generator*, of course, but was a remarkable achievement considering the relatively unfashionable nature of the music itself. This was not Yes 'dumbing down' for the 1980s; this was Jon Anderson's vision of his 'new Yes' – modern and retro at the same time – for better or for worse.

The first thing to correct were some legal issues surrounding how to use the word 'Yes' in any marketing for the album and tour. The Squire, White, Rabin and Kaye version of the band – 'Yes West' as it is known – were the 'official' Yes, and legal objections were raised at the outset. Brian Lane, as we were to see when the same issue arose with a different combination of musicians in 2017, was desperate for the sake of ticket sales to co-opt their old moniker if he could. In the end, the tour was to be by Anderson, Bruford, Wakeman, Howe playing 'An Evening of Yes Music plus'. Honour was satisfied and the duel was over. Bruford, however, was typically wary of some of the motivations behind the tour:

Call me slow, call me old fashioned. These things operate on a musical level first, and Jon had said Steve was going to be there and it all sounded great. But of course, there was a manager, Brian Lane. But the manager's job, not unreasonably, is to turn the thing into money somehow, and the only way you did that was by calling it Yes, or something very like Yes or 'an evening of Yes music' or something similar. So, pretty soon, it all started to sound like a reunion of the original Yes. In all fairness, I wasn't trapped. I could have got off the wheel, but these things are a bit incremental. Once you've made a record, it turns out you're going to be spoiling everyone's party if you don't participate in order to sell the record. It's a very strong tangible pressure upon you. Having said that, I could have got off if I'd wanted to, but I thought, 'bloody hell, let's do a summer tour with this.'

The tour itself received some notoriety beyond the music press, well before the album was even released. Indeed, there were many aspects of the tour which presaged ways of working more common with the 2020s than the 1980s. One thing you could always say about Brian Lane was that he knew how to do a deal. In his 'Bizarre' column in *The Sun*, former Sounds scribe Garry Bushell referred to a major sponsorship deal with as yet-unnamed American airline (later revealed, as the tour programme clearly shows, to be Continental). Confusion, at that stage, reigned over the name of the group, however, with Bushell clearly thinking that this was to be a Yes line up, with his article also mentioning various other rockstar trappings, such as 'a luxury 747 with jacuzzi.' Whether Bushell got the wrong end of the stick about the name or was fed something speculative is not known.

Chris Squire spoke to Mark Putterford of *Kerrang* on a rare visit to London in 1989, and his bitterness at the project was clearly evident, saying of Anderson and the band:

> I don't think he was that vital to the band [Yes]; our *90125* album, which was a huge success, was written before Jon rejoined, and he didn't get involved until the last two weeks of recording. And then during work on the *Big Generator* album, Jon became really hard to get on with, and consequently, the project took a long time to do. So, I think the atmosphere in the band will be a lot better now.
>
> And if they sell some back-catalogue records as a result, then I won't complain, that's for sure! But I don't know whether what they're doing will wash anywhere other than Britain. I mean, *90125* was massively successful everywhere in the world except Britain — and so I suppose there must be some people over here who thought we split up in the '70s. Maybe these people will go and see 'The Anderson Band' for old time's sake, but there's an awful lot of people who know that Yes is, in fact, me, Alan, Tony and Trevor.

Disingenuous this may be, but it's not hard to understand Squire's attitude. He may well have regretted saying that within the year, of course, but that's another story.

The ABWH tour began in July 1989 with a trek across North America (where the project *did* wash, of course), followed by Europe in the autumn. Indeed, on and off, the tour did not finish until March 1990 with a final jaunt to Japan, climaxing in a final, triumphant date at Madison Square Garden on 23 March 1990. The choice of venues was generally arenas, rather than theatres as might have been expected. It was a bold move of Lane to go for such venues, but it paid off and attendances were excellent. Bruford was astonished by the level of love for the band, describing their reception at the Spectrum arena in Philadelphia on August 3 1989:

[The response] produced the loudest sound I've ever heard. Deafening, sustained applause, which was far louder than the group. Back then, you could still offer a mixed set of 50-50 new material and old familiar music and still leave the stadium alive. When we finished 'And you and I', that continuing blast from the huge audience sounded like a jet engine warming up, I was genuinely moved by this gargantuan display of affection. The more so, because I had long forgotten how persuasive 20,000 throats could be.

The tour is well documented, mainly via the live album and video recording from Shoreline Amphiteater in California from 9 September 1989. For the sequence of concerts during which this recording was made, Bruford's other favourite bassist Jeff Berlin stood in for an ill Tony Levin, so it's his performance that most people have experienced. Thankfully, Levin was back in time for the UK dates in October, and several other performances were recorded both for audio and video.

Structurally, the musicians put together an interesting show, which has not been repeated since. It began with showcases for each of the four principals, making good use of backup musicians Milton McDonald on guitar and Julian Colbeck on keyboards. Anderson entered first, playing a well-chosen acoustic medley of 'Time and a Word', 'Teakbois' and 'Owner of a Lonely Heart'. Howe then played a two-track acoustic set – often 'The Clap' and 'Mood For A Day' – followed by Wakeman's medley of solo material. Bruford's trip around his electronic percussion took place in 'Long Distance Runaround' and then it was into an electric set which mixed the best of the new album with Yes songs from the Bruford era, including superb versions of 'Heart Of The Sunrise' and 'Close To The Edge'. This terrific shows saw a highly motivated band – a cynical Bruford notwithstanding – playing with great fire and commitment. The tour was a highpoint in their careers and is a favourite of many Yes fans that saw it (sadly, your author didn't).

'The Meeting' took on extra significance when the band played in Germany, in November 1989, at roughly the same time that the Berlin wall came down. It came to signify the meeting of East and West in Germany – a poignant and emotional time for the Germans.

Rick Wakeman – *Sea Airs*

Personnel:
Rick Wakeman: keyboards, composition, production
Released: 1989
Tracklisting: 1. Harbour Lights 2. The Pirate 3. Storm Clouds 4. Lost at Sea 5. The Mermaid 6. Waves 7. The Fisherman 8. Flying Fish 9. The Marie Celeste 10. Time and Tide 11. The Lone Sailor 12. The Sailor's Lament

Rick Wakeman and Mario Fasciano – *The Black Knights at the Court of Ferdinand IV*

Personnel:
Rick Wakeman: keyboards, composition
Dave Sumner: guitar
Mario Fasciano: drums, percussion, vocals, composition
Released 1989
Tracklisting: 1. Evuje' 2. Favola 3. Umberto II   4. Umbe' 5. Tommaso Aniello (Masaniello) 6. Fradiavolo 7. Farfarie 8. O' Bilancio

As a solo artist, Rick was entering a period where it was necessary to take whatever opportunities presented themselves, and he released two albums in 1989, neither of which are generally classed as classics, although both have a fair amount of interest for listeners. *Sea Airs* was the latest in a series of instrumental piano albums that Rick released around this time as *The Rick Wakeman New Age Collection*. Several progressive rock artists found new homes making this sort of music – Jon Anderson would also dip his toes in this water a few years later. Rick's album is lovely – if, once again, not especially memorable from a melodic point of view. However, several tracks do genuinely evoke the sea, and while Rick has admitted that other pieces found themselves on the album by accident, it served its purpose – to relax the listener once more – admirably.

The other album is a genuine curiosity, a recording in progressive rock style with Neapolitan musician Mario Fasciano, who plays drums and sings. Tonally, it's very much in the style of Italian prog bands like Banco, PFM and Le Orme. The lyrics are in Neapolitan Italian, so evoke that sort of vibe, and the singing of Fasciano is very much in that style too, while the melodies deliberately attempt to evoke the tone of the Italian Renaissance. It's partially successful, particularly as – despite his unmistakable playing – it doesn't really sound much like a Rick Wakeman solo album. As Rick has said, it's poorly produced and mixed, and (as he hasn't said) we find Rick once again in the middle of his 'questionable synth patch' period, so the noises he makes have dated somewhat, too. But if – like me – you'd previously never heard this album, it's worth 36 minutes of your time at least.

Steve Howe – *Turbulence*

Personnel:
Steve Howe: guitar, dobro, mandolin, koto, keyboards, percussion, bass, hurdy-gurdy, sequencing, arrangement, sound effects, engineering, production, composition
Billy Currie: keyboard, viola
Andrew Lucas: organ
Bill Bruford: drums
Nigel Glockler: drums
Roger Howorth: engineering
Tim Weidner: engineering
Croyden Cooke: engineering
Renny Hill: mixing
Recorded 1988/1989 at Hot Food Studios; Advision; Sarm East/West Studios; Langley Studio
Released 1991
Tracklisting: 1. Turbulence 2. Hint Hint 3. Running the Human Race 4. The Inner Battle 5. Novalis 6. Fine Line 7. Sensitive Chaos 8. Corkscrew 9. While Rome's Burning 10. From a Place Where Time Runs Slow

Although Steve's third solo album wasn't released until 1991 – in the wake of the Anderson. Bruford, Wakeman, Howe project – the majority of the recording took place after the dissolution of GTR (or what GTR became after Hackett's departure), so it's worth discussing briefly here, particularly in the light of how it influenced the *Union* record.

While many of Steve's albums since have been relatively low budget affairs and a mixture of rock and acoustic material, here Steve was clearly attempting something different, as evidenced in the recruitment of a big name 'band' of sorts, with Bill Bruford on drums and Ultravox's talented Billy Currie on keyboards. Indeed, this is largely an instrumental progressive rock album, with each of its ten tracks beautifully constructed and without all-acoustic diversions as there had been on *Beginnings* and *The Steve Howe Album*. Two of the tracks had instrumental sections that were specifically lifted for pieces on *Union*. 'The Inner Battle' was to become 'Silent Talking' and 'Sensitive Chaos' was to become 'I Would Have Waited Forever', although the versions on Howe's album are arguably better developed. Elsewhere, there are some finely crafted pieces, especially the lovely 'Corkscrew' and another fan favourite in 'Running the Human Race' featuring some beautiful steel guitar, and first demoed as a GTR-era piece sung by Max Bacon.

Recorded at Advison and Sarm East and West, and finished at Hot Food Studios in Notting Hill, it was a hugely ambitious – and presumably expensive – project that showed Steve working at a level that would rarely be repeated after that point. That it was released on a small independent three years after it was recorded must have been disappointing.

Trevor Rabin – *Can't Look Away*

Personnel:

Trevor Rabin: lead vocals, guitar, guitar synthesizer, keyboard, bass, background vocals, engineering, production

Lou Molino III: drums

Alan White: drums

Denny Fongheiser: drums

"Basil": drum machine

Duncan Faure: background vocals

Tsidii Le Loka: background vocals

Beulah Hashe: background vocals

Faith Kekana: background vocals

Marilyn Nokwe: background vocals

Bob Ezrin: background vocals, engineering, production

Released 10 July 1989

Highest chart places: USA: 111

Tracklisting: 1. I Can't Look Away (Rabin,Ezrin, Anthony Moore) 2. Something to Hold on To (Rabin) 3. Sorrow (Your Heart) (Rabin) 4. Cover Up (Rabin, Godfrey Rabin, Moore) 5. Promises (Rabin) 6. Etoile Noir [nb 1] (instrumental) (Rabin) 7. Eyes of Love (Rabin, Ezrin) 8.I Didn't Think It Would Last (Rabin, Ezrin) 9. Hold on to Me (Rabin, Patric van Blerk) 10. Sludge (instrumental) (Rabin) 11. I Miss You Now (Rabin) 12. The Cape (instrumental) (Rabin)

With his Yes commitments complete for the time being, Rabin decided to restart his solo career, signing a deal with Elektra records. As with Anderson and *City of Angels*, this must – on the face of it – have seemed a natural development. He was, after all, the author of a number one single plus several other hits. To cement the importance of his next solo project, Bob Ezrin was brought in to co-produce with Rabin.

Ezrin, as we've already seen, is not just a knob-twiddler, though unlike many producers, he is also an excellent engineer. Those that have seen how he related to the bands with whom he works – and there's some excellent footage of him working with Deep Purple during the last few years – will understand that he gets intimately involved in the creation of the music itself particularly regarding tone and arrangement. Also – and this is crucial – he won't have come cheap. This was no side project. Elektra expected a hit album.

The production vibe that Ezrin often creates on his many projects with (for instance) Alice Cooper and Pink Floyd, are much in evidence here. There's a bombastic feel to much more of the material than was present on Rabin's earlier three albums produced in the late 1970s. There are also a lot of effects (like the megaphone effect on the first verse of the title track) and percussive quirks produced by 'Basil' – a drum machine, of sorts. Meanwhile, the drum sound – whether played by long-time cohort Lou Molino III, Alan White or session man Denny Fongheiser – booms in late 80s style.

In fact, looking at it now, it's an odd album in terms of tone. It opens with 'Can't Look Away' which is certainly an epic, but with a lengthy guitar outro that makes it feel like an album closer. In a largely positive in-depth review on the *Yes Music Podcast* in 2020, presenters Kevin Mulryne and Mark Anthony K disagreed on where the album falls down (if indeed it does), Kevin suggesting that it had one too many of the bombastic rock tracks, while Mark pointed his criticism at the three quirky instrumental pieces, 'Sludge', 'Etoile Noir' and 'The Cape'. At 55 minutes, it's not a long album by CD-era standards, yet the quirky track sequencing, and some arguable 'sameyness' amongst the rock tracks – largely due to Rabin's one-paced songwriting when viewed across an entire album – give the album an unusual feel.

Rabin's experience over the past few years had certainly given his songwriting more maturity, although it could be argued that this maturity didn't come to its full fruition until the Yes album *Talk* in 1994. The three instrumentals hint at interests that weren't to be fully indulged until his instrumental *Jacaranda* solo album in 2012. Fans of his two Yes albums to that point (and indeed *Talk*) will probably find much to like, here. Fans of 1970s Yes will find a lot less. The songwriting is largely good but lacking a killer instinct or obvious hit, while Rabin's lyric writing is fairly bland – 'love' orientated and lacking in depth. 'Something To Hold On To' is catchy and the label must have smelled a hit there, and while it performed well in the *Billboard* mainstream rock chart, and its video was Grammy-nominated, it didn't cross over into the pop charts as several Rabin-penned Yes songs had done in living memory. In short, the album is missing a 'Owner of A Lonely Heart' or a 'Love Will Find A Way'.

One gratifying development was Rabin's use of four South African backing vocalists on several songs, most notably the excellent 'Sorrow (Your Heart)' which borrows the rhythms and textures of South Africa music for its verse before a more conventional chorus. This is the first time that Trevor had used such textures in his own music, although Rabin – a cousin of activist Donald Woods (the journalist and subject of the movie *Cry Freedom*) – had long been an opposer of the Apartheid regime. Despite some criticism at the time, mainly from anti-apartheid campaigners who maintained that a zero-contact policy was most likely to end the regime, Paul Simon's *Graceland* album had been released three years earlier, to massive success. This made working with black South African musicians both morally and commercially acceptable and gave Rabin the ability to follow suit.

In the main, though, this was a stadium rock album that appeared at a time when such music was starting to become tired, in the eyes of the buying public, if nothing else. Although the album stayed on the *Billboard* chart for ten weeks, a placing of 113 must have been a considerable disappointment for the label. There was to be no immediate follow-up. The following year, grunge would find its first commercial success and the stadium rock world would go into stasis...

The last action by anyone in the wider Yes alumni at the end of the decade was a short US solo tour by Rabin – playing clubs and small theatres. Most of the show at The Roxy in LA on December 13 1989 was released in 2003. It's worth a listen. As well as songs from *Can't Look Away*, the tour set also included one song from his previous solo album *Wolf*, and some Yes pieces, played fairly faithfully, in 'Changes', 'Love Will Find A Way' and 'Owner Of A Lonely Heart', which featured lead vocals by the audience. Interestingly, the show intro tape was the introduction to 'Lift Me up', to appear on the ill-fated *Union*. One wonders how well advanced in the recording process that song was at the time. It was to become a part of yet another new era for Yes...

..and for the rest...?

Given the amount of time that Anderson, Bruford, Wakeman, Howe spent on tour during 1989, and the high profile of the album, there was little or no solo activity from the other participants. We do, however, have four other musicians to consider. Yes certainly still existed, but with the jolt of Anderson's departure, the musicians began to work with other participants. Initially, there was talk of Roger Hodgson of Supertramp taking over as lead vocalist in Yes – a move that the label were certainly interested in, due to his profile as a hitmaker with Supertramp, and, of course, his high register voice. Rabin did some writing with him, and one track was to appear on Yes' 1994 album *Talk*. Squire formed a fruitful relationship with multi-instrumentalist Billy Sherwood, which was to become deeper as the 1990s progressed. We'll let Mark Putterford of Kerrang finish the story for us, with the help of Chris Squire, once again discussing the fortunes of 'Yes West' against 'the others' – namely ABWH:

When Rabin is free, they'll steam straight into recording (possibly with producer Eddie Offord, who worked on several of the early Yes classics such as *Yessongs*; that's if the 'others' don't get to him first!), and then, after resolving the lead singer situation, they intend to hit the road, and could possibly play some British dates before the end of the year.
'I suppose it'll be interesting to see how things develop from here,' concedes Squire, 'but I don't regard them as rivals or anything; we're in competition with them only as much as we are with anyone who releases a record. Yes will continue regardless until . . . well, until the music runs out. And it certainly hasn't yet!'

It certainly hadn't.

Into the 1990s and beyond – 'I'm not hearing a hit...'

Anderson, Bruford, Wakeman, Howe – with a successful album and a triumphant tour under their belts – now needed to produce a second record. There was always a problem, in that while Anderson had been working on the material for the first album for years, now an album needed to be created from scratch. Indeed, Anderson even reached out to Trevor Rabin for material. But 'the suits' had other ideas. Bruford again distils the situation that the band found themselves in very succinctly in his autobiography. It's a sorry tale:

> Arista executive Roy Lott who had dreamed up this nightmarish scenario with [Brian} Lane, was the man holding the purse strings, and he soon started calling the shots. The whole smorgasbord was to be presided over by producer Jonathan Elias who would make regular reports on whether this bunch of miscreants was making the kind of record, not what that the musicians wanted, but that Arista thought it could sell. Rough demos of progress were Fedexed to the headquarters in New York City and soon messages were coming back with the suits along the lines of: 'more tambourine on the bridge' or 'I'm not hearing a hit'. Allowing the record company to create the music is about as wise as allowing the musician to look after the money. And around this point, any experienced musician knows that all is lost. Will the last person out turn off the light?

Essentially, a plot had been dreamed up between Arista executive Ray Liott and Brian Lane that the next album would be made by an amalgam of all the musicians that laid claim to being associated with Yes but working in two camps. However, there would be some cross-pollination between the two groups, which essentially (in the end) boiled down to Anderson providing some lead and backing vocals to the 'Yes West' material and Squire adding some backing vocals to the ABWH tracks (on which Tony Levin still played bass). It was half-hearted stuff.

To sort out the mess of the ABWH material, producer and composer Jonathan Elias was brought in to produce the album. Howe says that this was Anderson's choice, although it's likely that Elias was appointed both by Anderson and Arista. Yes historian Henry Potts interviewed Elias about what he found in 2001. Elias pulls no punches, and his readers are requested to take a deep breath before reading this crucial part of his testimony:

There was no material. Basically, what there was Steve [Howe] was working on a solo album [later released as *Turbulence*] and he brought in some things. Jon [Anderson] brought in one or two faint ideas. I couldn't get these guys to sit down and write material without other people being in the room because of the social reasons. They had just been on the road for so many years and they probably had so many episodes with each other. Half of them couldn't really play anymore. I mean, it was really sad. They were just sloppy and tired and old.

These guys were barely 40, let's not forget. One suspects that if the musicians had been left to their own devices and – crucially – offered a level of respect that seems to be missing in Elias' attitude, a better product might have come about in the end. Aside from the addition of some vocals by Anderson, the Yes West tracks were presented largely as they had been recorded, and offer a rather better standard, even if there are something of a mishmash of styles, producers and personnel. In a move that smacks of Squire's 'return to the mean' policy first utilised on *Drama*, Eddie Offord was given another opportunity to make his mark with the band, and Billy Sherwood made his first appearance on a Yes album.

The ABWH songs were finished – in a hurry – with the participation of an army of session players. As a result, Wakeman can barely be heard on the album and many of Howe's parts were replaced by other musicians. The *Union* album was released in the middle of 1991, to unhappy reviews and mediocre sales. Almost all of the band – particularly Howe, Wakeman and Bruford – have disowned the album, although it has seen some reassessment in the intervening 30 years. It's certainly not all bad, but the ABWH tracks are underdeveloped and a few of the Yes West songs – 'Saving My Heart' being an obvious example – don't feel like they belonged on a Yes album at all.

The subsequent tour – despite some personality clashes (Howe and Rabin, mainly; musical rather than personal, it would seem) – was triumphant. Played in the round, as the 1978 *Tormato* had been, the eight-man lineup wowed audiences worldwide through 1991, although the sheer number of musicians meant that the number of solo spots took up a fair amount of each show's running time. 'Terrible album, great tour' seemed to be the consensus.

But the drama was not yet over. With Bruford never likely to hang around after his contractual obligations were at an end, Howe and finally Wakeman were dropped, leaving the *90125* lineup once again holding the baton. In truth, however, *Union* was the last album that saw Yes treated as a major label act with sizeable production and promotional budgets. While 1994's *Talk* was a largely successful collaboration (at last) between the talents of Anderson and Rabin, it was released on the short-lived Victory label, fronted by old friend Phil Carson. Despite the link to Japanese tech giant JVC, the label was not a success, and the album did not fare well. If the 1980s had been all about survival and success against the odds, the 1990s onwards saw various versions of the band – with Howe and Wakeman both returning and Wakeman, in particular, in and out on what felt like a yearly basis – lurching from opportunity to opportunity, dragged as much as anything by cash on the table.

The Ladder, released in 1999, was the band's last hurrah as an album-tour-style recording outfit, with the subsequent set the last to feature a substantial amount of new material. 2003 saw the band's 35th anniversary and some renewed media interest as well as a compilation album *The Ultimate Yes* that did well commercially. Thereafter, while new albums have appeared from time to time with gradually diminishing returns financially, the touring band became something of a heritage act, concentrating on 'classic' material. Two major tours in 2003 and 2004 notwithstanding, Yes have become a part-time band, with its various members also concentrating on solo careers, even other bands, with Howe taking part in a reformation of the original lineup of Asia.

The crucial lineup change took place in 2007, when a proposed tour with Rick's son Oliver on keyboards was postponed due to a serious illness to Anderson. The band elected eventually to carry on with different singers – first Benoit David and then Jon Davidson. Anderson – once recovered – teamed up with Rick Wakeman as a duo and then formed a rival band with Wakeman and Trevor Rabin – whose career in the meantime had moved into the production of movie soundtracks.

Meanwhile, Yes fans and his band members alike were rocked by the premature death of Chris Squire in 2015. With Alan White unable to play as he once had and in the band as much as a talisman as anything, the band – with the Anderson rival version now seemingly dissolved – retains is credibility through the presence of Howe as leader and the participation of Geoff Downes and Billy Sherwood, whose past involvements in the band are crucial to its credibility, on keyboards and bass respectively.

The Legacy of a Crazy Decade

There's nothing that a certain sector of the Yes community like more than to speculate about 'what might have been' concerning Yes in the 1980s. It's impossible to such speculation without disappearing down a rabbit hole of interesting, even entertaining – but probably futile – alternative realities.

Much of the band's music recorded during the 1980s has stood the test of time. The *Drama* album was rehabilitated following the ousting of Anderson in 2008, with first 'Tempus Fugit' and 'Machine Messiah' in the set, and then the rest of the album for tours shortly after Squire's death. Without Anderson in the band, the album has regained its status with some of the classic 1970s albums in terms of stature. Some would say quite right too.

The status of *90125* has varied, depending on who's in the band at any given time. Steve Howe has reluctantly played 'Owner of A Lonely Heart' on and off for years, although at the time of writing, it feels as far away from a Yes live set as it was before it was created. The Anderson, Rabin, Wakeman version of Yes understandably played a fair chunk of *90125* on its 2017/2018 tours, but failed to delve into *Big Generator* in the same way – only 'Rhythm Of Love' getting the nod. 'Rhythm', ironically, was the one 1980s era track that the Howe version of the band has played with any sort of enthusiasm, the song a mainstay of the 2004 world tour. Anderson plays 'Owner' in his live shows and also maintains a sweet but slightly strange attachment to 'Love Will Find Away', a song he did not write and on which he did not sing the lead vocal.

Circumstances mean that almost all the material created on the ABWH album is unlikely to see the light of day again unless Howe has an unlikely change of approach. 'Birthright' at least surely needs to be heard in a live setting. Meanwhile, Asia have continued. The long-lived John Payne and Geoff Downes version stopped suddenly following the reformation of the original lineup in the late 2000s and then with new members (including Billy Sherwood) following Wetton's untimely death in 2017.

There's little doubt that the 1970s and 1980s versions of the band made their music in very different environments. In the 1970s, even although labels were as interested in record sales as much as they were a decade later (and are now), the way of achieving this was more orientated towards artist development. But one of the recurring phrases in this book is 'I'm not hearing a hit', and from the late 1970s onwards, throughout the 1980s, this was the mantra of every record executive working for a major label, hit singles being considered the fastest way to success and to profit. Both Yes, and all of its members in their solo and other-band endeavours throughout the decade, heard variations on this phrase time and time again. Even Rick Wakeman.

That Yes were able to survive at all must be considered a miracle. But survive, the band did.

Horn, who still loves *90125* – changed perspective on the *Yes Classic Artists* documentary – and took a moment to consider the sensibilities of the 1970s Yes fan and what his reaction to *90125* might have been:

I don't know if I'd have liked it. I'd have liked some of it. But I'd see parts of it is coping out and selling out to some sort of stadium rock ethic that I wouldn't have approved of.

The straight-talking Australian Mike Tait has some sympathy with that view that still excises Yes fans almost forty years later, saying in the same documentary:

'Owner of a Lonely Heart' with Trevor Rabin and everything to me was nothing. It was a pop song. I couldn't care less. They could have had studio musicians doing that. It wasn't Yes. There was nothing right about it.

Rick Wakeman is equally blunt about it, but from a different perspective:

Many yes fans consider *90125* and *Big Generator* not to be true Yes. I can understand that because those two albums are a different genre of music entirely. But to me. It saved Yes' life. There is no doubt about it.

We'll leave the final word to Alan White. In typically stoic, diplomatic and balanced fashion, he gives his perspective. He's talking about *Drama*, but he could be discussing the whole decade. I, for one, agree with him:

I think Yes fans, in general, accepted the idea that we wanted to further the career of the band. And just respected us for doing that.

Bibliography

Books
Welch, C., *Close To The Edge – The Story Of Yes* (Omnibus Press, 1998)
Popoff, M., *Time and a Word – The Yes Story* (Soundcheck Books, 2016)
Watkinson, D., *Yes – Perpetual Change* (Plexus, 2001)
Bruford, W., *The Autobiography* (Jawbone, 2009)
Morse, T., *Yes Stories – Yes In Their Own Words* (St. Martin's Griffin, 1996)
Chambers, S., *Yes – An Endless Dream Of '70s, '80s And '90s Rock Music* (General Store, 2002)
Wakeman, R., *Say Yes* (Hodder And Stoughton, 1995)
Lambe, S., *Yes On Track* (Sonicbond, 2018)
Dancha, Kim., *My Own Time – The Authorized Biography of John Wetton* (North Line, 1997)
Howe, Steve., *All My Yesterdays* (Omnibus, 2020)
Hewitt, Alan., *Sketches Of Hackett – The Authorised Steve Hackett Biography* (Wymer, 2009)

Magazine Resources
Prog magazine (various articles and interviews)
Rock Candy magazine (issue 23)

Sleeve Notes
Dome, Malcolm., Jon Anderson *Song of Seven* sleeve notes – Esoteric Reissue (2020)
Dome, Malcolm., Jon Anderson *Animation* sleeve notes – Esoteric Reissue (2021)
Smith, Sid., *Anderson Bruford, Wakeman, Howe* – Esoteric Reissue (2014)

Videos
Yes Classic Artists documentary (Black Hill DVD, 2008)
Yesyears documentary (Warner VHS 1991)

Online resources
yesworld.com – the official Yes website
yesfans.com – long running fan site and forum
yesmusicpodcast.com – excellent weekly podcast about the band
bondegezou.co.uk – website of long-term Yes chronicler Henry Potts
forgotten-yesterdays.com – invaluable online resource
rwcc.com – Rick Wakeman's official website
progarchives.com – essential progressive rock archive and review site

On Track series

Barclay James Harvest – Keith and Monica Domone 978-1-78952-067-5
The Beatles – Andrew Wild 978-1-78952-009-5
The Beatles Solo 1969-1980 – Andrew Wild 978-1-78952-030-9
Blue Oyster Cult – Jacob Holm-Lupo 978-1-78952-007-1
Kate Bush – Bill Thomas 978-1-78952-097-2
The Clash – Nick Assirati 978-1-78952-077-4
Crosby, Stills and Nash – Andrew Wild 978-1-78952-039-2
Deep Purple and Rainbow 1968-79 – Steve Pilkington 978-1-78952-002-6
Dire Straits – Andrew Wild 978-1-78952-044-6
Dream Theater – Jordan Blum 978-1-78952-050-7
Emerson Lake and Palmer – Mike Goode 978-1-78952-000-2
Fairport Convention – Kevan Furbank 978-1-78952-051-4
Genesis – Stuart MacFarlane 978-1-78952-005-7
Gentle Giant – Gary Steel 978-1-78952-058-3
Hawkwind – Duncan Harris 978-1-78952-052-1
Iron Maiden – Steve Pilkington 978-1-78952-061-3
Jethro Tull – Jordan Blum 978-1-78952-016-3
Elton John in the 1970s – Peter Kearns 978-1-78952-034-7
Gong – Kevan Furbank 978-1-78952-082-8
Iron Maiden – Steve Pilkington 978-1-78952-061-3
Judas Priest – John Tucker 978-1-78952-018-7
Kansas – Kevin Cummings 978-1-78952-057-6
Aimee Mann – Jez Rowden 978-1-78952-036-1
Joni Mitchell – Peter Kearns 978-1-78952-081-1
The Moody Blues – Geoffrey Feakes 978-1-78952-042-2
Mike Oldfield – Ryan Yard 978-1-78952-060-6
Queen – Andrew Wild 978-1-78952-003-3
Renaissance – David Detmer 978-1-78952-062-0
The Rolling Stones 1963-80 – Steve Pilkington 978-1-78952-017-0
Steely Dan – Jez Rowden 978-1-78952-043-9
Thin Lizzy – Graeme Stroud 978-1-78952-064-4
Toto – Jacob Holm-Lupo 978-1-78952-019-4
U2 – Eoghan Lyng 978-1-78952-078-1
UFO – Richard James 978-1-78952-073-6
The Who – Geoffrey Feakes 978-1-78952-076-7
Roy Wood and the Move – James R Turner 978-1-78952-008-8
Van Der Graaf Generator – Dan Coffey 978-1-78952-031-6
Yes – Stephen Lambe 978-1-78952-001-9
Frank Zappa 1966 to 1979 – Eric Benac 978-1-78952-033-0
10CC – Peter Kearns 978-1-78952-054-5